T0274098

Your Way to
TRUE
WEALTH

Your Way to
TRUE
WEALTH

HOW TO MAKE IT HAPPEN,
MAKE IT LAST,
AND MAKE IT MATTER

MIKE BROWN

GREENLEAF
BOOK GROUP PRESS

Published by Greenleaf Book Group Press
Austin, Texas
www.gbgpress.com

Investment advisory services offered through Raymond James Financial Services Advisors, Inc. Brown Family Wealth Advisors is not a registered broker/dealer and is independent of Raymond James Financial Services. Securities offered through Raymond James Financial Services, Inc., member FINRA/SIPC.

Brown Family Wealth Advisors
165 North Meramec Avenue, Suite 200
St. Louis, Missouri 63105

314.571.9897

Distributed by Greenleaf Book Group

For ordering information or special discounts for bulk purchases, please contact Greenleaf Book Group at PO Box 91869, Austin, TX 78709, 512.891.6100.

Design and composition by Greenleaf Book Group and Mimi Bark
Cover design by Greenleaf Book Group and Mimi Bark
Cover image used under license from ©Shutterstock.com/memphisslim

Publisher's Cataloging-in-Publication data is available.

Print ISBN: 979-8-88645-054-5

eBook ISBN: 979-8-88645-055-2

To offset the number of trees consumed in the printing of our books, Greenleaf donates a portion of the proceeds from each printing to the Arbor Day Foundation. Greenleaf Book Group has replaced over 50,000 trees since 2007.

Printed in the United States of America on acid-free paper

23 24 25 26 27 28 29 30   10 9 8 7 6 5 4 3 2 1

First Edition

To Tammy Thompson Brown, my partner in life and business, my wife, and my soulmate: You made me truly wealthy long before we had two nickels to rub together.

CONTENTS

WHAT A DAY
THAT WOULD BE

I would like you to imagine a very special day. It's the day you wake up and realize that:

FROM NOW ON, WORK IS OPTIONAL. No alarm clocks, no rush-hour traffic, no mandatory meetings, no one telling you what to do and when to do it. If you choose to work, it would be at something that gives you joy and purpose. Or you move on to something more fulfilling. Either way, you don't work for money anymore—because you don't need to.

YOUR INCOME HASN'T STOPPED. YOU'RE still receiving enough money each month to pay for the lifestyle you have chosen, and that income is increasing over time at least as rapidly as your cost of living. The only difference is that you no longer have to go out and work for it.

YOU ARE INDEBTED TO NO ONE. That's right; no mortgage, no car payments, no credit card balances carried over from the month before. You are completely debt free and will stay that way for the rest of your life.

YOU DON'T WORRY ABOUT MONEY ANYMORE. You no longer have fears about what the financial markets are doing, anxieties over the latest economic forecasts, or doubts about making your money last as long as you need it to. These worries are behind you.

YOU NO LONGER WASTE PRECIOUS TIME ON THINGS THAT DON'T MATTER. You have stopped trying to predict the future and listening to the predictions of other people you think are smarter than you. You've quit reacting to the alarmists and fearmongers who dominate the financial media. You no longer measure your investment success against arbitrary market indexes.

YOU SPEND YOUR LIFE ON THINGS THAT *DO* MATTER. Teaching a child how to play shortstop, helping grandchildren afford college without borrowing, ensuring financial security for your spouse, leaving a legacy of wealth and wisdom to successive generations.

What a day that would be.

I gather by the look on your face right now that this day hasn't arrived for you just yet. That's okay. You and I are getting ready to take the first steps on a path toward what I call True Wealth. And if what I have just described appeals to you, the book you are holding could help you get there.

What a day that *will* be!

HOW MOST PEOPLE DEFINE WEALTH

Would you rather be the smartest person in the world but have everyone think you're the dumbest—or would you rather be the dumbest person in the world but have everyone think you're the smartest?

Your answer to that question will tell you a lot about yourself. Famed investor Warren Buffett says human beings measure themselves either by an "inner scorecard" or an "outer scorecard." We either set standards for ourselves, or we let the world set those standards for us.

I grew up in North Carolina, where the state motto is *Esse Quam Videri*, a Latin phrase that means "to be rather than to seem," but today I live in a world where people spend hours online each day trying to convince their former high school classmates that they are richer, happier, and more successful than they really are.

They believe wealth is how much money you make, your income.

They believe wealth is how much money you have, your net worth—or what neighborhood you live in, or what your house looks like, or what kind of car you drive, or what clubs you belong to, or how you dress, or where your kids go to school, or where you go on vacation, or how recently you upgraded your cell phone.

They believe wealth is how well your investments are performing relative to the S&P 500 or some other arbitrary benchmark. Or simply whether your 401(k) account grew faster than your brother-in-law's did last quarter.

Those are all *outer scorecard* measurements. They are someone else's definition of wealth. But they're not mine, and if I can convince you to think a little differently, these things won't be your definition of wealth, either.

True Wealth is neither your income nor the value of your possessions. It doesn't involve a number that once reached will make your financial future forever secure. In fact, it cannot be measured with any outer scorecard. So, what exactly is it?

True Wealth is the point in
your life at which you no longer
have to work for money.

This is not a complex idea, but actually *achieving* True Wealth is anything but easy. Most people never do, and there's no guarantee you will be successful. But know this: Whether you get halfway there, 90 percent there, or all the way there, you will be far better off financially—almost from the start—than you would have been otherwise. Every step you take toward this goal will make the next one easier, and the new habits you develop along the way will begin to redound to your benefit almost immediately.

If you choose to embark on this journey, there are three things to understand.

The first is that your assets alone cannot make you financially independent, but your *income* can. For example, if it costs X-thousand dollars a month to live exactly the way you want to live, and X-thousand dollars gets deposited into your checking account on the first of every month, then the size of your portfolio doesn't seem overly important, does it?

Second, whether the income comes to you in the form of a pension, Social Security benefits, rental income, interest, or dividends isn't terribly important, either. What does matter is that it's *passive* income, something you don't have to go and earn with your time and effort when you would rather be doing something else.

Third, this income needs to be: (1) *sufficient* to support the lifestyle you've chosen; (2) *consistent* and reliable; and (3) *increasing* at least as rapidly over time as your cost of living.

Always remember that True Wealth is measured with an inner scorecard—*your* scorecard. You get to decide what lifestyle is important to you. You will figure out how much it will cost each year. You will be able to add up how much passive income you are receiving—today or in the future—and know how close you are to True Wealth.

Obviously there are only two ways to get there: either by increasing the income you receive or by decreasing your need for it. Of course, you will always have much more control over what you *spend* than what you *earn*, so focusing most of your efforts there is much more likely to help you succeed.

Because you are still reading, I'll assume that the idea of being able to define wealth on your own terms has some appeal to you. I will also assume that you're not exactly where you want to be financially at this point.

You might just be starting out in life, looking for a plan to take you from zero net worth all the way to True Wealth. Maybe your net worth today is even *less* than zero, and you need a plan just to dig your way out to the starting line. Or perhaps you're farther along in your journey. It's possible you've reached True Wealth already without even knowing it. Even if that's the case, you need a plan to keep you there, so that you can continue to enjoy life *beyond* True Wealth.

Let me make something else clear right from the start. Nothing in this plan will require you to systematically liquidate your life's savings to pay your bills once you stop working, hoping that you won't outlive your money. However you choose to define True Wealth and the income it will take to achieve it, I want you to be able to maintain your chosen lifestyle *on just the income your investments generate,* supplemented by whatever you ultimately receive from Social Security, pensions, and any other passive income sources.

If instead you prefer to spend as much of your life's savings as possible once you stop working, you might be able to reach True Wealth even sooner and spend more each year after you get there. If that's your goal, this book also contains guidelines to help you avoid spending too much of your nest egg too soon.

Whatever your definition of True Wealth, or wherever you begin your journey toward and beyond it, there's a plan within these pages to help you get there.

WHAT YOU AND I LIKELY HAVE IN COMMON

True confession: My career as a financial role model had less than auspicious beginnings.

For starters, I was not born into wealth. When I was five years old, my dad traded in a successful sales career and what little savings he and my mother had for a general store in the country that lasted less than five years. He lost his dream of entrepreneurial independence and his family along with it. Pop died alone without a nickel to his name two weeks after my 28th birthday.

I didn't marry into wealth, either. When Tammy and I bought our first home, we asked her father to lend us the down payment. He politely refused, saying we would be better off in the long run by figuring out how to come up with the money on our own. And he was right: He taught us to get out of debt as early as possible, and we've been able to live that way for most of our adult lives.

Like you, I've never won the lottery despite having bought a ticket on at least two occasions. Turns out that's a good thing, because nobody seems to have more trouble hanging onto money than professional athletes and lotto millionaires.

If you're anything like me, I'm guessing that whatever money you have didn't come from blind luck but from hard work. And whatever you've saved is the result of a conscious decision at some point—likely thousands of them—not to spend it when you could have.

However, I've always been interested in money, not so much with the intention of getting rich but for the independence it makes possible. Working my way through college not only allowed me to graduate without student loans, but it also covered Tammy's and my dating expenses. She and her college roommate still laugh at the thought of me reading Sylvia Porter on their lumpy apartment couch while they sat on the floor watching *Mork and Mindy*.

My curiosity led me to more reading and more study. My love of words took me into a career in journalism and jobs in radio, newspapers, and television, and over time I developed a following among people who wanted to learn about investing and personal finance. Eventually, I left journalism behind and started helping those people directly as their financial advisor. Nearly three decades later, many of those people are still my clients, as are their children and some of their *children's* children.

Tammy left behind a successful career in accounting to join me early on, and our only child, Adam, joined the practice two years out of college, just in time to witness the Global Financial Crisis of 2007–2008. Our daughter-in-law, Vicki, joined the family business in 2017. Today, we help hardworking people define True Wealth, achieve it, and then enjoy it for the rest of their lives.

It is for those clients—and at their urging—that I wrote this book. They've adopted its ideas, principles, and strategies for their own benefit, and they wanted a step-by-step guide to share the process with people they care about. They don't buy into the convenient claim that the system is somehow rigged and that True Wealth is reserved for the fortunate few, and neither do I.

I believe that if you have the ability to earn a living, the discipline to live within that income, and the patience to let your savings compound over time, you will one day be able to live off the income your investments produce while keeping your principal largely intact.

Regardless of where you are on your journey to True Wealth—however long the rest of this journey might take—if you want to get there, I will show you the way. I can't promise that it will be easy or quick, but I see people achieving True Wealth all the time.

Here's a preview of what to expect in this book:

- We'll begin by focusing on **three key concepts.**

- I'll pass along **seven guiding principles** to help you on your journey.

- I will point out **seven potential obstacles** that could knock you off your path if you're not prepared for them.

- I'll outline step-by-step plans for **building** wealth, for **transitioning** into True Wealth, and for **making wealth last.**

- And finally, I've created some important **mileposts** to track your progress.

One last thing: This book is not an academic thesis; it's a *user's manual.* It's not full of theories and formulas and ideas that *should* work. It's about principles and habits and strategies that *have* worked since before you and I were born.

It's time now for you to start learning these things, putting them into practice—and reaping the benefits you deserve.

CHAPTER 1

THREE KEY CONCEPTS

The first step to achieving True Wealth involves understanding three key concepts. They'll underpin everything else we discuss in the following pages.

CONCEPT #1: Success

Let's begin by what we mean by the term "success." How should we define it? How will you know when you've achieved it?

Here are a few suggestions on what success is—and what it isn't.

Success is not *luck*; it's *design*. Luck is owning a winning lottery ticket. Success is never feeling the need to buy one in the first place. Being lucky is not the same as succeeding; likewise, being successful does not require luck. Successful people have no interest in waiting around for good fortune to come their way; they spend their time creating their own opportunities. Truth be told, one of the worst things that can happen to you as a new investor is to get lucky on your first transaction, because novices often confuse beginner's luck with skill.

You can actually go out and create your own luck by learning what to do and doing it repeatedly. And if you *were* lucky enough to be born on third base, good for you. Just don't go through life thinking you hit a triple.

Success is not a *destination*; it's a *habit*. It's actually a *series* of good habits cultivated over a lifetime, small but important things that you are willing and committed to doing over and over again. History is full of examples of successful people—athletes, musicians, business owners— who rose to the tops of their professions by mastering the fundamentals and applying them repeatedly.

Good habits take longer and are harder to acquire than bad habits, and their benefits may only become evident over time. But they can help you succeed financially and become a better person in the process. When it comes to money, doing the small but right things day after day, month after month, year after year will allow you to incrementally build wealth until success—True Wealth—is yours.

Success is not having *more*; it's having *enough*. True Wealth is based on the premise that you—*and you alone*—have the ability to define it, based on the lifestyle you choose and the level of income you require to support it. That's different than saying, "I want to be rich" or desiring to have more material goods than other people. It's recognizing the point at which you have *enough* to satisfy your own needs and wants. You should never have to settle for less than that, and nothing will require you to keep going beyond whatever it takes to achieve it.

In his poem, "Joe Heller," Kurt Vonnegut recalls attending a party on New York's Shelter Island given by a wealthy hedge fund manager. Vonnegut asks his friend and fellow author Joseph Heller, "Joe, how does it make you feel to know that our host only yesterday may have made more money than your novel *Catch-22* has earned in its entire history?"

To which Heller responds: "I've got something he can never have."

"What on earth could that be, Joe?"

"And Joe said, 'The knowledge that I've got enough.'"

You have the right, the ability, and the freedom at this moment to decide exactly how much is enough. The more lavish your wants, the more money you will need and the longer it will take to acquire it. If your wants are more modest, you will likely reach your goal sooner. Just remember that it's *your* definition of success we're working toward and that there will never be a need to satisfy or even acknowledge anyone else's.

CONCEPT #2: Responsibility

So far, everything you've read should be good news:

1. You don't need luck to achieve True Wealth.

2. It's possible for you to create wealth by cultivating some simple habits and applying them consistently over time— habits you will soon learn.

3. You get to define what constitutes True Wealth, on your own terms.

Now the hard reality.

The price that financial freedom demands from you is that you also accept full responsibility for your actions and the results they produce. In short, this is all on you.

You must accept the difficult truth that nobody owes you anything. Not your parents. Not the government. And certainly not the financial markets. You won't get good results just because you need them.

You must also accept the fact that financial success—as with every other kind—requires work. As poet Robert Frost put it: "The world is full of willing people—some willing to work, the rest willing to let them." I realize how corny this sounds, but it's true.

When you accept full responsibility for your actions and their results, you also agree to stop measuring yourself against other people. Envy is not an attractive trait, nor is it a viable investment strategy.

Complaining won't help, either. It's been said that most of the people you know aren't actually interested in your problems, and the rest are glad that you have them.

So, here's the arrangement I propose: I will teach you the principles and strategies you will need to help you succeed financially. And I will help you put them into everyday practice with a proven plan that you can follow for the rest of your life.

You get to define success on your own terms. *You* get to do the work. *You* get to accept responsibility for the outcome. And *you* get to reap *all* the rewards and take *all* the credit.

Does that sound fair enough to you?

CONCEPT #3: Wisdom

There is a lot of free financial advice available to you these days, and it's worth every penny.

A tiny amount of what you read and hear might actually apply to your situation and have some value. Much of the rest is probably well-meaning and harmless but of limited use. A lot of the financial information you come across every day is misleading or simply wrong. And, unfortunately, some of it is actually malicious and meant to take your money and do you harm.

We all want people to tell us the truth, but truth alone isn't wisdom. Wisdom only *begins* with truth.

In your search for financial wisdom, it will help if you can distinguish that from everything else that whizzes past your eyes and ears each day. You won't encounter real wisdom very often, even when you're looking for it. To help you recognize it when you see it, a visualization might help.

Imagine a three-dimensional pyramid with four horizontal layers, each roughly the same thickness. The bottom layer is the largest and easiest to access; you can walk right up to it from any direction. What you will find there is an endless collection of numbers, statistics, and other raw materials. We will call this lowest level of the pyramid **data**. Financial data is abundant, free, instantly and constantly accessible, and, on its own, practically worthless. Data has no meaning—and no real value—until it is assembled into another form and given context.

When that happens, the data becomes **information**, which resides on the second layer of the pyramid. Getting to this level takes a little more effort on your part. Information is less abundant than raw data and therefore of greater potential value. When you organize data into information, it can be used to make informed decisions. But information alone gives little if any advantage to you personally, if for no other reason than that it's also readily available to everyone else. When it comes to investing, for example, you must assume that public information—what you hear on the news or see online—is already known and has been acted upon by the investment community. As legendary investor Bernard Baruch observed, something that everyone knows isn't worth anything. If there's any advantage to be had from information alone, it might be in recognizing a truth that other investors *don't* see or choose to ignore.

This brings us to a third and even smaller level, higher up on the pyramid, which we will call **knowledge**. Knowledge is far less plentiful than data or information. It takes more time and effort to reach this level, but what you will find here will likely be of greater value. Knowledge is more than simply knowing things, however; it's *understanding* what those things mean and how they might be of use to you. You've heard it said that "knowledge is power," but that's not entirely true. Knowledge only has power when it is successfully acted upon. There is the knowing, and there is the doing. Big difference.

In the end, what we seek resides on the tiniest level of the pyramid, all the way at the very top. It takes a lot of climbing to reach it, and most people seem to quit before they get there. Yet this is where we find **wisdom**, a rare, precious, and often expensive commodity. Once you acquire real wisdom, it belongs to you forever—or until you choose to ignore it.

Wisdom is knowing what to do with the knowledge you have accumulated and using it to a good end. It means taking advantage of what you've learned and the experience you've gained to make better decisions, both with your finances and with other aspects of your life. Wisdom often comes disguised in brief, insightful, but simple phrases.

> "Knowledge is a process of piling up facts; wisdom lies in their simplification."
> —MARTIN H. FISCHER

One very important final point before we move on: Wisdom means more than using what you know to make better decisions; it also means recognizing that *some things are not knowable*. For example, we can't know if the markets will be higher or lower tomorrow, what the rate of inflation will be next year, or which party will win the next election. Thankfully, financial success doesn't require us to know those things.

As an investor, you will learn a great deal from both your successes and your failures, and you will base most of your future decisions on what you have learned in the past. But you will also have to base some of those decisions on things that you accept as unknowable.

We've now packed your travel bag with a few essential ideas. Let's move on now to the seven basic but essential principles that will help guide you on your journey to True Wealth.

TAKEAWAYS

- You know the meaning of financial **success**, and you understand that the term is yours alone to define.

- You accept that in exchange for the right to define success on your own terms, you must also accept all of the **responsibility** for the decisions you make.

- And you understand that **wisdom** comes not from facts, figures, or formulas, but from knowing what to do with the knowledge and experience you acquire, and then acting on it.

CHAPTER 2

SEVEN GUIDING PRINCIPLES

As you pursue True Wealth, there are things that will help you along in your journey—*Seven Guiding Principles*—and things that will hold you back—*Seven Potential Distractions.*

You will soon notice that the Principles are all *internal* traits. They are qualities or beliefs that you either already possess or that you can develop over time. The Distractions, in contrast, are largely *external* forces that threaten to negatively impact the way you think about money and the actions you take in response to those obstacles. Those we will cover in the next chapter.

PRINCIPLE #1: Behaving Yourself

Like many people, you might still be laboring under the misconception that financial success is largely determined by how much money you invest, which investments you select, and when you decide to buy and sell them.

You might be surprised (and somewhat relieved), however, to hear that your success won't likely come from any of those factors. In fact, the key to investing has very little to do with *investments* at all—and almost everything to do with *investors*.

In short, it's all about *you*. Or more specifically, your behavior.

> "The dominant determinant of long-term, real-life financial outcomes isn't investment performance; it's investor behavior."
> —NICK MURRAY

Industry studies, such as the annual *Quantitative Analysis of Investor Behavior* from the financial research firm DALBAR, Inc., consistently show that individual investors tend to underperform the very investments they own. How is this possible? It happens largely because more money seems to come into the financial markets when prices are relatively high and rising, and greater sums leave the markets when prices fall. That's the exact opposite of buying low and selling high, something even novice investors understand is the key to profits. Actually doing that, however, is easier said than done, mostly because of human emotions.

It can be a little disheartening when you realize for the first time that you are your own worst enemy, but it can also be liberating. Think of it this way: If you are the problem, then you can also become the solution. If you can recognize and accept your shortcomings, you can do something about them and perhaps even turn them to your advantage.

Think of the last time you shopped for groceries, researched a new laptop, or purchased a new home or car. Recall how good it felt when something you wanted to buy went on sale. It's perfectly rational to see lower prices as an opportunity. We all love a bargain—and even brag about how much money we saved—with one notable exception.

When stock prices drop 20 or 30 percent, our brain tells us to run the other way.

It would appear we all come from the factory wired backward on this one. When it comes to investments, our tendency is to associate falling prices with higher risk—the risk we might lose money—and to feel more comfortable and confident as prices rise. In truth, the opposite is generally true: There is a positive correlation between prices and risk, yet it's difficult to remain calm and rational when everyone around you is stampeding for the exits.

It's perfectly natural to experience emotions; it's what makes us human. Successful investors, however, may find that it's more productive to act in opposition to the way we feel. For example, it's okay to feel concerned when you're told a severe economic recession is coming or that the next bear market could be right around the corner. But as an investor it's almost always a mistake to *act* on those emotions. We will explore this further in later chapters, but for now just remember these three things:

1. The key to your financial success is your own behavior.

2. You will always experience emotions and be tempted to act in response to them.

3. Financial success depends on your ability to act *counter* to the way you feel.

As I've pointed out, success involves a series of good habits, and you will soon learn some specific habits for overcoming your human instincts and keeping your emotions in check. For now, just realize that your behavior will have far greater impact on your results than the investments you choose or how the markets perform. Accepting full responsibility for your own behavior is the first step toward getting the results that you want.

PRINCIPLE #2: Faith in the Future

Someday in the not-too-distant future, the next genius entrepreneur will drop out of Harvard and share a bold new idea with the rest of the world. And somewhere in a part of that world that you and I have never visited, someone will wake up tomorrow morning with a desire to be more than they are today, to do more for their family, and make their tiny corner of the world a better place.

We live in a world that—through our own collective efforts and those of others before us—continues to get better. Most of the time, however, we are unable to see that, and even if we do, we've been conditioned to view the evidence with suspicion. Bad news sells, and way too many of us are buying it.

> "One thing alone I charge you. As you live, believe in life! Always human beings will live and progress to greater, broader, and fuller life. The only possible death is to lose belief in this truth simply because the great end comes slowly, because time is long."
> —W. E. B. DUBOIS

Positive proof of such progress is all around us. Over the past century, humans have gotten healthier, richer, smarter, and freer. We are living longer, more productive lives, which is leading to economic growth throughout the developed world. That productivity continues to drive down global poverty rates. Education is better and more accessible; literacy rates are rising. Despite depressions, wars, and pandemics that temporarily slow or even reverse them, these long-term trends seem to somehow persist. People continue to think, to experiment, and to reap the benefits of their own ideas and initiative. And there is every reason to believe that this progress will continue, never in a straight line, never without interruption, but never in doubt.

If you agree, then you might just be able to align yourself with this continuing progress. If not, I believe you're going to have a hard time becoming financially successful. You won't prosper in a world or among a people that you don't believe in. Pessimism is a lousy investment strategy.

To be a good investor, it helps to have faith in yourself and faith in the future. Not a blind faith, clearly. Not a wild-eyed belief that success is somehow guaranteed or that things won't occasionally go wrong along the way. A degree of skepticism—a bit of caution when warranted—will help you in many ways. But understanding that optimism based upon evidence is the only realism will help you even more.

> "The intelligent investor is a realist who sells to optimists and buys from pessimists."
> —BENJAMIN GRAHAM

These are the good old days you'll tell your grandkids about one day. There has never been a better time to be alive.

PRINCIPLE #3: Thinking Differently

All of your life you undoubtedly have been taught to study and think about things until you understand them. When you succeed, something clicks, and you say to yourself: "This *makes sense* to me now. I understand why this is true."

As you learn more about investing, however, you will sometimes have to come to a different conclusion: "This *doesn't make sense*; it's not in any way logical. But under some circumstances it might *still be true*." See the difference?

A lot of investment truths don't make sense on the surface, no matter how much you try to understand them. Once you accept that something can be true even though it doesn't make sense, however, you will save yourself a lot of time and trouble.

> "I'm convinced that everything that's important in investing is counterintuitive—and everything that's obvious is wrong."
> —HOWARD MARKS

Science, medicine, and engineering are all based on performing specific actions and expecting consistent results based on empirical evidence. If you demand proof before you invest, however, you will never be a good investor, because investing is about the future, and you can't prove something that hasn't happened yet.

When it comes to investing, logic and reason often take a backseat to emotion. Facts and data are essential in making good investment decisions, but in the short run at least, it's the collective, often illogical response of investors to those facts and figures (and other less objective inputs) that determine *prices*. Day-to-day prices of securities—and therefore market averages as a whole—are driven by emotions, which is why it's impossible to consistently predict them over the short run.

Consider a few common examples:

- Bad companies sometimes turn out to be good investments.

- Disappointing economic news can trigger stock market rallies.

- Times of crisis—economic, political, or societal—are often the best time to invest.

- Falling prices might *feel* risky, when, in fact, risk is declining and potential increasing, all else being equal.

Investing is a world where good news is sometimes bad, and bad news is occasionally good. Results are often determined not by the facts at hand but by *expectations* of what's to come. Things can happen for what appear to be the wrong reasons and, just as often, for no apparent reason whatsoever.

Investing successfully, then, often means doing things that don't make sense at the time.

That's why you get better prices when you buy straw hats in the winter and snow shovels in July, when no one else needs or wants them. And, in my opinion, it's also why you should aggressively seek out investment opportunities when the overall outlook is bleakest and be more cautious and skeptical when conditions seem perfect.

Always remember this: Investing is not about what's happening now but what will happen *next*. And most of the time, of course, we simply don't know what that might be. That's why it's often a mistake to invest based purely on today's headlines.

We can't know the future, and we can't invest entirely on what we know about the present. That means that a lot of the time we'll need to do things that don't feel right and then wait for our decisions to possibly be validated in the future. With no guarantees, the best we can hope for is to put the odds of success solidly in our favor.

Today's comfort comes at a high cost, and tomorrow's rewards come from doing what most other investors won't.

PRINCIPLE #4: Simplicity

The problem with humans isn't just that we often fall prey to our emotions; it's that we also seem to have a perverse desire to make things more complicated than they need to be. Complexity can create the illusion of intelligence, while simplicity can imply ignorance or naiveté. Let's face it: Being described as "simple-minded" is not a compliment.

To a novice, investing seems very complex. It has its own terminology and jargon, and it tends to focus largely on events that haven't happened yet. That complexity may sound intriguing, even sophisticated.

Yet many of history's most accomplished investors downplay the importance of genius or even above-average intelligence when it comes to creating wealth. Warren Buffett once said that success in investing stops correlating with IQ above the level of 25. Beyond ordinary intelligence, he observed, what you need is the temperament to overcome the urges that get many investors in trouble.

If you are seeking investment wisdom, you will often find it camouflaged in simplicity.

> "The greatest paradox of this remarkable age is that the more complex the world around us becomes, the more simplicity we must seek in order to realize our financial goals. Never underrate either the majesty of simplicity or its proven effectiveness as a long-term strategy for productive investing. Simplicity, indeed, is the master key to financial success."
> —JOHN C. BOGLE

If genius is the rare ability to take the complex and make it simple, then investment genius requires the confidence to be suspicious of overly complex ideas and strategies. It also requires the humility to focus on simple actions that work: save, invest, compound, repeat.

I've seen people roll their eyes when I tell them that building wealth through investing is based on a handful of very basic, elementary ideas. And yet these same people will continue through life struggling financially, searching for complex answers to simple problems without even considering that the answers to their fiscal worries lie in the wisdom of simplicity. They think "it can't possibly be that simple," and yet it is.

I suspect these folks are looking for financial success in complex ideas and formulas. They never realize that success comes not simply from knowing but also from *acting* on a few basic truths. Once you understand them, you simply keep doing them over and over while resisting the temptation to make your work more complicated than it needs to be.

PRINCIPLE #5: Self-Discipline

Doing the same things over and over again requires self-discipline. And self-discipline means doing what you *should* be doing, even when you would prefer to be doing something different.

The good news is that successful investing does not require superior intelligence. It's not about being smarter than everyone else but having enough common sense to stick with what works.

> "I used to think being great at investing was about genius . . . Genius is good, but more and more I think it's about doing something reasonable, that makes sense, and then sticking to it with incredible fortitude through the tough times."
>
> **—CLIFF ASNESS**

Self-discipline acts as a counterbalance to the emotions that threaten your ability to make wise decisions with your money. Faith in the future might help you keep your emotions at bay, but discipline is what will allow you to consistently act in opposition to the way you feel. And we've already seen that investing often involves doing the opposite of what feels natural and normal.

Finally, self-discipline means sticking with your beliefs and continuing to act on them *even when you're not getting the results you want.* We will soon highlight some time-tested strategies that have worked well for investors. But no matter how successful these strategies may have been, there are always periods of time—sometimes lengthy stretches—when they seem to stop working. Those are the times when your faith, patience, and discipline will be put to the test.

Having a good strategy is vital, and there are many effective investment approaches. But no strategy works *all of the time.* The key to long-term success is not necessarily which strategy you choose but how well you're able to continue following it when other approaches appear, in the moment at least, to be working better than yours.

Even a mediocre strategy that you are able to stick with when times get tough will likely be far superior to an ingenious one that you abandon at the first sign of trouble. And it will take some discipline on your part to do that.

PRINCIPLE #6: Patience and Time

> **"The two most powerful warriors are patience and time."**
> **—LEO TOLSTOY**

Time is what brings you the rewards that you earn from self-discipline. And patience is the trait that allows you to wait for time to work its magic.

The next chapter of this book describes several distractions that will threaten to knock you off the path to True Wealth. They will always be there waiting to tempt you. The sooner you are able to recognize them, the better you'll be able to ignore them. And the best way to do that is by maintaining a long-term focus on your goal of financial independence. You will have short-term goals, of course, and they will help lay the groundwork for your bigger goals, but both require patience.

Time is the essential ingredient in making money grow and compound. Time is a big part of what creates investment returns, and the process cannot be rushed, no matter how much we would like to hurry it along.

> "Virtually all investing mistakes are rooted in people looking at long-term market returns and saying, 'That's nice, but can I have it faster?'"
> **—MORGAN HOUSEL**

It's been said that the stock market is a mechanism for transferring wealth from the impatient to the patient. If you want to be an *investor*—as opposed to a trader or speculator—you must believe that long-term returns are the only ones that matter and abandon the notion that short-term returns are of much importance. Clearly, there is money to be made in trading and speculation, but if that is your goal, you are reading the wrong book.

Short-term investing is an oxymoron.

There is a simpler way to make money grow, and it takes a lot less work. What it *does* require is time. And enough patience and self-discipline to stick around long enough for your strategy to work. As you'll discover when we discuss the mechanics behind compounding investments later in this book, money itself can do most of the hard work if you are simply patient enough to let it happen.

PRINCIPLE #7: Having a Plan

When our son, Adam, was very young, I helped coach his baseball team. One point that we constantly drove home with the kids was the importance of deciding—*before* every pitch—exactly what they would do if the ball was hit their way.

We taught each player to have a plan. I can still hear my little shortstop say, "Catch the ball, then check the runner on second. If he runs toward me, I'll tag him. If he doesn't, I'll throw to first base and get the batter out." It was simple: Catch the ball. Check the runner. Throw to first. And then, of course, look for your mom in the stands to make sure she saw the play.

In so many aspects of life, it's important to know how to react to events and situations in the right way. Even more important is making a plan *beforehand* to help make sure things turn out the way you want them to.

The sea captain sets a course based on a chosen destination, accepting the fact that he or she has no control over conditions—winds, currents, storms. They simply anticipate the response to changing conditions *without trying to predict the future with precision.* The captain knows how to sail as well as every task the crew needs to perform to safely reach the next port. They have a plan, they *act* on that plan, and then they adjust to events as they occur in order to stay on course.

> "It is the set of the sails—not the direction of the winds—that determines which way we will go."
> **—NAPOLEON HILL**

Your journey to True Wealth is very similar. You might believe it's the investments you choose, or when you buy and sell them, that will be the key to your success. But investments are merely the vehicle that will help take you to your goal. Like those of the sea captain, the decisions you make when changing conditions threaten to push you off course will largely determine the success of your journey. Without a plan, there is no course to follow and no way to know when you've lost your bearings or how to recover them.

In short, you won't make it without a plan.

Setting goals is the first step. Then comes an honest assessment of where you stand financially and what resources you possess now and in the future. Next comes deciding what strategies you will use to move you forward. And the final step in planning is to lay out a series of mileposts, calculating where you will need to be—and by when—to reach your destination on schedule.

Only when the plan is in place should you consider how best to invest. You don't buy a river canoe first and *then* try to figure out if you can cross the ocean with it. Plan the voyage, *then* select the right boat. Make a plan for True Wealth first, and then start saving and investing.

Once your plan is in place, your portfolio designed, and your journey set to begin, you'll need to decide how you will respond when things don't go the way you planned, because the one thing you can count on is that they won't.

"You get recessions, you have stock market declines. If you don't understand that's going to happen, then you're not ready. You won't do well in the markets. If you go to Minnesota in January, you know it's going to be cold. You don't panic when the thermometer falls below zero."

—PETER LYNCH

Knowing how you will likely feel—and then what you will do in response—when something threatens your financial success is the key to your plan. Imagine thinking: *I just bought my first stock. Bad news came out the very next day, and the price fell 10%. I feel like I've been punched in the stomach, but I'm not going to panic. I'm going to review my research, and if I still like what I see, I might even buy more shares.*

Catch the ball. Check the runner. Throw to first. That's the plan.

This book contains a plan that you can adapt to your own needs and desires. It will help you plot a course to True Wealth however you define that. It includes step-by-step instructions followed by a set of mileposts to help you stay on course. But you must remember that your success will ultimately be determined not by how your investments perform relative to some arbitrary benchmark, but by whether you reach the destination you've chosen.

Competing with market averages is using an outer scorecard. It's not even a worthy goal, much less a plan.

TAKEAWAYS:
THE SEVEN GUIDING PRINCIPLES

1. Behaving yourself

2. Faith in the future

3. Thinking differently

4. Simplicity

5. Self-discipline

6. Patience and time

7. Having a plan

CHAPTER 3

SEVEN POTENTIAL DISTRACTIONS

You now have a basic understanding of the guiding principles that will help you in your journey to True Wealth. But there will be many distractions along the way, and every single one of them has the potential to trip you up, divert you from the path, delay your progress, or stop you in your tracks. The better you understand these distractions, the more quickly you will recognize them—not if, but when you encounter them.

DISTRACTION #1: Fear

You already know that the greatest threat to your success is located within you, because you are a human being and subject to human emotions. The most dangerous of these emotions is fear. Fear is a basic human instinct, programmed into our DNA to keep us alive and safe.

Fear can be pervasive and contagious, and in an oddly human way we are often attracted to it. We slow down to gawk at automobile accidents. We watch horror movies and we jump out of perfectly good airplanes for fun. Advertisers know our human tendencies and play on our fears in order to sell us things. The news media use fear to get us to pay attention and boost their audiences. And why is it that we are often more interested in what the doomsayers are shouting than the calming voice of those with a reasoned, optimistic outlook on things?

Fear is natural and, in some cases, even healthy. It's when fear reaches *extremes* that it gets us into trouble. Over time, fear can turn into pessimism, which, unchecked, becomes gloom and dread. When the things investors fear actually start happening—which occurs less often than you'd think—fear can even turn into panic. And panic almost always triggers bad investment decisions.

> "The psychologists tell us that fear is more contagious than any other emotion, and there is probably no place where fear does more damage than in the securities markets."
> **—THOMAS GIBSON**

The problem with fear and pessimism—while real and perhaps even potentially warranted in the short term—is that they are generally not supported by the evidence over the long haul. Investors have been warned countless times that the end of the world is near, yet it has never happened. On the contrary, the history of the human race is one of continued improvement, innovation, and accomplishment. For thousands of years the march of progress has been ever upward, ever onward—and ever ignored by those who remain convinced that bad times await us all.

As an investor, you must overcome the fears you will inevitably face when sudden market drops temporarily turn your hard-won profits into losses. But how?

Begin by understanding what market declines truly are: scary events that happen fairly frequently but not according to any schedule. They are also typically brief in duration. The fact that prices can be volatile and unpredictable is actually what gives certain investments their superior returns. When markets get scary, acknowledge your fears, feel them, *and then refuse to act on them.*

As you evolve as an investor, you may even be able to turn fear to your advantage. You will understand all the things you cannot control: the economy, market volatility, taxes, what has happened in the past, what will happen in the future. And you will learn to narrow your focus to the handful of things that you *can* control, such as your response to outside events or, better yet, how you choose *not* to respond.

Whatever your current view of the world, I believe you will discover at some point the essential truth that things are never quite as bad—or even quite as good—as they seem.

DISTRACTION #2: Greed and Envy

Greed is fear's alter ego. Together, these two basic human emotions are likely more responsible for the money lost in market extremes than any other factor.

The goal of investing, naturally, is to earn a return on your money in the form of income, capital appreciation, or perhaps both. History gives us an idea of what returns we might reasonably expect over time, but sometimes our expectations surpass reason. As with fear, there are many catalysts that can spark excessive optimism, which in turn can lead to greed: a technological development that changes the world, for example—the printing press, railroads, the internet—or it could be something as mundane as a prolonged bull market.

When human beings get truly excited about something, especially something as appealing as a new opportunity to make themselves money, that excitement becomes contagious. If people we know seem to be making lots of money, we naturally want to find out how. We want to participate and not be left out. After all, why shouldn't we do as well as they do?

Soon someone reminds us that opportunities never last for long and must be seized before they vanish. What began as curiosity turns to envy, and envy then becomes a different kind of fear: the fear of missing out (FOMO).

> "Nothing so undermines your financial judgement
> as the sight of your neighbor getting rich."
> —J. P. MORGAN

Greed is ever present, and in a free-market society its milder forms can be a motivating force for progress. But like fear, when greed reaches extremes, it becomes dangerous. When investors feel too good about an idea for too long, their excitement can turn into collective euphoria, a general feeling that things are different this time and that the old rules no longer apply. When you start believing that risk is no longer present, that the more things go up the less likely they are to come down, that the good times will last forever, or that you've got to get in before it's too late, you have crossed into dangerous territory.

When you purchase an investment simply because its price has gone up, you're subscribing to the "greater fool" theory, which says it doesn't matter what you pay for an investment because there will always be an even greater fool willing to pay you a higher price for it when you decide to sell. At this point you are no longer an investor but a speculator.

When the markets deliver above-average returns and you're disappointed that yours aren't even higher, your inner scorecard has become an outer scorecard, and you have set yourself up for even greater disappointment down the road.

Fear and greed both tend to build slowly and gradually. It will take a while for you to acknowledge the influence they are gaining over your decisions, but once they take hold of your thinking, they are difficult to overcome. Unless you do so, however, they will threaten your financial success and delay your journey to True Wealth.

When you feel these emotions creeping in, go back to your plan. Feel grateful when your returns are higher than expected, and then temper your expectations about the future. Revisit the lessons you're now learning.

> "Investing isn't about beating others at their game. It's about controlling yourself at your own game."
> —BENJAMIN GRAHAM

DISTRACTION #3: Shortsighted Thinking

I still remember a cool summer morning the year before I turned 16. I was behind the wheel of a moving car for the first time ever, trying to learn how to drive. With my fists firmly clenched in the nine and three o'clock positions, I kept my gaze fixed on the pavement no more than ten feet beyond the hood ornament, nervously nudging the steering wheel from side to side every few seconds in an effort to maintain my course. At that point Mr. Wilson, the junior varsity football coach and driver's ed instructor sitting in the passenger seat, gave me a driving tip that I'll never forget. "Lift up your head," he said. "*Look farther down the road where you want to go,* and you won't need to jerk the wheel so often. Just slow down. Stay calm. Relax. And try your best not to get us all killed."

Coach Wilson wasn't much of a confidence booster, but he helped me pass my driver's test. And although I didn't know it at the time, his advice ultimately made me a much better investor.

Most of what you see and hear in the financial media deals with short-term events and developments, and their importance (if any) is magnified in order to grab your attention. Yet a lot of what seems so urgent today will wind up being completely irrelevant by tomorrow. If what you see and hear elicits an emotional response in you and you choose to react to it, you may wind up regretting your decision. The shorter your focus, the more likely you are to *overreact* and make a mistake.

> "Do you know what investing for the long run but listening to market news every day is like? It's like a man walking up a big hill with a yo-yo and keeping his eyes fixed on the yo-yo instead of the hill."
> —ALAN ABELSON

Like a yo-yo, market prices go up and down constantly, and too many investors fail to focus on anything else. They begin to see trends and patterns where none exist. They confuse background noise with meaningful information. They *react* to market volatility instead of acting on their plan. They never see past the hood ornament and wind up running off the road.

My advice to you is to keep your attention focused on your destination, on the road instead of the shoulder, on the hill instead of the yo-yo. Base your investment decisions on their long-term implications, not on what might or might not happen tomorrow. Thinking this way will become easier for you as you gain experience and perspective.

And be careful about the kind of information you consume every day. If it's wisdom you seek, you'll have a much better chance of finding it in a history book than a newspaper.

DISTRACTION #4: The Media

I hate being the one to break this to you, but you should hear it from a friend with firsthand experience: Those affable folks who tell you how the markets did today, and why, and what might happen tomorrow (unless of course it doesn't) *have no vested interest whatsoever in whether you succeed or fail financially.*

They don't know who you are. They don't know your goals, your investing experience, your age, or your tolerance for risk. They don't know the first thing about you, but that doesn't stop them from telling you how to invest your life's savings. And if they tell you the complete opposite tomorrow or next week, well, so be it.

As I've said, shortsighted thinking is a hazard to long-term investors, and financial journalism has elevated shortsightedness to an art form.

As purveyors of raw data and ever-changing information, every hour brings the opportunity for "breaking news" and updated commentary from an endless carousel of "experts" and pundits. Exciting news means more viewers, more eyeballs, more clicks. That means better ratings, happier advertisers, and higher profits.

But what's in this for you?

> "Understand that CNBC wants to make you poor and stupid. Turn it off—that's the first thing you can do. The second thing you can do is learn some financial history."
> **—WILLIAM BERNSTEIN**

Extremely good or bad news tempts you to respond emotionally and encourages you to take action, even when acting isn't in your best interest. Fear and greed sell equally well.

At its very best, the media can help you make more informed decisions that contribute to your success. At its worst, you miss context, perspective, and sometimes even truth. Sadly, much of what we see, hear, and read every day has become increasingly biased and agenda driven. And that agenda has little to do with helping you become financially secure.

It's one thing to use the financial media as a source of information.

Consume it at your own risk. You should never rely on it as a source of unquestioned wisdom nor let it distract you on your journey to True Wealth.

DISTRACTION #5: Politics

The United States operates under a political system of democracy: one *person*, one vote. At the same time, it operates under an economic system of capitalism: one *dollar*, one vote. Democracy is based on the idea that all citizens deserve equal opportunity under the law. Capitalism is based on the idea that each of us has the right to use that opportunity to pursue financial success to whatever extent—and by whatever legal means—we choose.

Neither system is perfect, and both have serious shortcomings, but no one has yet come up with anything else that's close to the benefits they provide. And despite some built-in conflicts, democracy and capitalism have been able to coexist.

As a citizen of our country, you are bound by democracy's rules. And yet, while our nation was founded on the promise of equal opportunity, neither democracy nor capitalism guarantees equal outcomes.

> "Capitalism doesn't know about or care about fairness in the sense of equal sharing. What it considers fair is the proposition that people who have greater ability or work harder should be able to earn more. That potential, it says, provides incentives for hard work and rewards those who achieve, ultimately resulting in a better life for almost everyone."
> —HOWARD MARKS

No matter how smart you are or how hard you work, no one can guarantee that you will succeed financially. If you agree to do the work and accept full responsibility for your results, you should expect to reap the rewards. That's how free enterprise works: no limits to financial success, and no guarantee against failure. And if at first you don't succeed, as the saying goes, there's nothing to stop you from trying again.

Democracy allows us to choose our leaders, and we are legally obligated to abide by the decisions they make. From time to time, you are likely to feel the political tide shifting away from you: Someone wants to raise your taxes, threaten your livelihood, or in some other way make it more difficult for you to succeed. That may make you frustrated and angry, and you can choose to act on that by voting your conscience and getting involved in political causes if you feel strongly enough.

But never make the mistake of mixing politics with investing.

Don't make major financial decisions based on who's in office, or who you would *like* to be in office, or who you fear might be in office after the next election.

There are two good reasons to keep your politics and your personal finances separate. The first is that the more strongly you feel about something, and the more closely you base your investment decisions on those beliefs, the more you will narrow your range of opportunities. Political biases, however justified, limit the odds of your financial success.

The second reason is that many of your fears and concerns about new leaders and new policies may never be realized. The founding fathers created an ingenious system of checks and balances to prevent too much power from being concentrated in too few people for too long. As a result, democracy moves slowly, big proposed changes shrink through compromise, and permanent consequences become temporary. The investment mistakes you make by overreacting to your fears and concerns, however, can easily and quickly result in permanent financial losses.

It's often said that politics is like a pendulum that swings back and forth, never stopping in the middle. Recognize and treat politics as a distraction, and don't let it knock you off the path to True Wealth.

And, finally, acknowledge that paying taxes is the price of your financial success. They support the system that makes it possible for you to succeed. Realize that the only thing worse than having to pay taxes is being in such a poor financial condition that you *don't* have to pay them.

Take full advantage of legitimate ways to reduce the taxes you owe, but don't arrange your entire financial life around these strategies. Understand the tax implications of your investment choices, but do not make them your primary consideration.

DISTRACTION #6: Predicting the Future

If all you knew about investing came from reading, watching, and listening to the financial media, you might think that your success is based on how accurately you can predict the future. And you might even come to believe that some people have a knack for it.

A certain forecaster sees economic trouble on the horizon and predicts that a major market decline is imminent. He turns out to be prophetic: Stock prices fall more than 30% across the board within days of his prediction, and a few months later the economy topples into recession. The forecaster is hailed as a genius and develops a celebrity following as Wall Street's latest guru. He is interviewed day and night as financial journalists breathlessly await his next pronouncement. You and countless other investors wonder why you didn't heed his warning and get out of the market when you had the chance.

But upon doing some further research, you discover this guru has been predicting market disasters almost daily for last decade. If you had been following his advice, there's a good chance you wouldn't have had any money left to *take* out of the market. On this occasion, however, his timing was perfect. As the saying goes, *even a broken clock is right twice a day.* The financial world is now hanging on the genius's every word, but no one has bothered to check his track record.

Why not? Because something inside us wants to believe that the future is knowable. We feel that surely some brilliant person—a statistics professor, a hedge fund manager, an astrologer—will finally crack the code and open the door to riches for those of us smart enough to pay attention.

Let me tell you something I've learned from studying the world's most successful investors. These are people who have been able to produce impressive and consistent returns over decades, each in different ways. And without exception, every one of them has a logical, well-organized philosophy for making investment decisions. Each also has the discipline to stick with his or her beliefs through the most challenging conditions.

None of these legendary investors, however, spends a lot of time trying to predict the future. It's not that they couldn't do a better job of it than the rest of us, it's because they realize that successful investing *doesn't require* knowing the future.

The sad irony is that some investment professionals will privately concede that they have no idea where the economy or the markets are heading next, but in order to make a living they need to have us *believe* that they do. They're the ones you're likely to see on cable shows.

> "There are two kinds of forecasters: those who don't know, and those who don't know they don't know."
> —JOHN KENNETH GALBRAITH

As an investor, you will be faced with the temptation to try outsmarting other investors—that is, "the market"—by anticipating its future direction. You'll hear some dire forecast about the next correction or bear market, and you'll start to wonder if you can somehow avoid it by selling your stocks and sitting in a less volatile investment like cash until the storm has passed. It's easy to think that way when times are difficult, and it's even easier to liquidate your entire portfolio with a single phone call or double click. That's called *timing the market,* and it could be one of the biggest investment mistakes you ever make.

There are at least three big problems with market timing:

1. No one—repeat, *no one*—has ever done it successfully and consistently.

2. It requires you to be right, not once but *twice,* every time you attempt it. Selling stocks is easy to do, especially when it relieves the pain of a falling market. The hard part is buying back in before prices fully recover.

3. Most importantly, market timing interrupts the wealth-building power of *compounding.* Without it, your goal of True Wealth moves farther and farther away from you.

You will never need to predict the future in order to reach True Wealth. You won't need to have a market outlook or pay attention to anyone else's. And you *certainly* won't need to run the fool's errand of trying to predict when is best to buy and sell your investments.

> "Far more money has been lost by investors preparing for corrections or trying to anticipate corrections than has been lost in corrections themselves."
> **—PETER LYNCH**

Instead, spend your time on things that truly matter. Don't predict the future, plan for it.

DISTRACTION #7: Dwelling on Mistakes

You are going to make some mistakes in your pursuit of True Wealth, no matter how well you learn these lessons or how well you apply them.

Realize there will be small missteps for certain but probably a few whoppers too.

And that's a good thing.

You see, the best way to learn about saving and investing is by doing it—with real money—and probably the worst thing that can happen to you is to be lucky with your first transaction. Success, especially the instant kind, is a poor teacher, because it tempts you to believe you are smarter than you really are and that you might be somehow immune from making bad decisions and losing money in the future.

It's much more likely that you will do extensive research on your first investment and convince yourself of its merits. You'll justify the price you are paying as attractive. After careful consideration, you'll buy a few shares, and then the price will drop right after you buy it. How do I know this? Because the same thing has happened to seasoned professional investors—people like me who do this for a living—every day.

The best investors have a much better idea of how their decisions will pan out over the next five years than what might happen in the next five minutes. You've already learned that the more time you give an investment or a strategy to work, the more likely it will come close to meeting your expectations. But that doesn't mean unexpected things won't happen along the way; that's one of the few things you can truly count on.

If your first investment purchase drops in price, that might simply be the result of random, short-term market fluctuations that are beyond your control. The yo-yo might simply be down that day. That's not a mistake; that's volatility. Get used to it.

On the other hand, you might realize over time that your investment thesis was flawed and that your investment decision was a poor one. Even the most successful investors make mistakes from time to time; you might get used to that as well.

The good news is that every poor financial decision can teach you something if you are smart enough to figure out what it is. So, when you lose, don't lose the lesson.

"In school, you're taught a lesson and then given a test. In life,
you're given a test that teaches you a lesson."
—TOM BODETT

Your biggest financial mistakes will probably not involve which securities you choose nor when you decide to buy and sell them. The big, punishing mistakes happen when you act against your own self-interest by ignoring timeless lessons. To avoid the big errors, master the basics—the fundamentals. Stop looking for what's working right now, and start paying attention to what has worked over time. Learn the right things to do, and then keep doing them—over and over again.

Don't second-guess your decisions, and don't dwell on your mistakes. Learn from them and keep going.

TAKEAWAYS:
THE SEVEN POTENTIAL OBSTACLES

1. Fear

2. Greed and envy

3. Shortsighted thinking

4. The media

5. Politics

6. Predicting the future

7. Dwelling on mistakes

CHAPTER 4

FIRST STEPS TOWARD TRUE WEALTH

"Whatever you can do, or dream you can, begin it.
Boldness has genius, power, and magic in it. Begin it now."

—JOHANN WOLFGANG VON GOETHE

We are going to start our journey to True Wealth at the absolute beginning, and we're going to start it now. Perhaps you've already been saving and investing for a while and want to skip ahead a few chapters. That's fine, but I would encourage you to stay patient and keep reading. You might just discover a key idea you've missed, and I assure you that a quick review of the fundamentals won't waste your time.

Of course, simply learning these ideas won't make you any better off financially any more than learning about cooking will make you a chef. At the end of the day, your success will be determined not by what you *know* but by what you *do*—and keep doing. You must put these lessons into practice and put your money to work.

And the sooner you start, the better.

START WHERE YOU ARE . . . RIGHT NOW

Don't wait for the right time to begin your journey. Don't wait for divine inspiration or for conditions to be perfect. If you need motivation, motivate yourself—you are taking responsibility for this, remember? As a matter of fact, you don't even need to share with anyone that you've decided to create a much better financial life for yourself and your family. It's time to just do it.

It doesn't matter how much money you *make*, how much money you *have*, or how much money you *owe* at this moment—and it shouldn't matter a great deal to you, either. What really matters is what you choose to do about it.

IT *DOES* TAKE MONEY TO MAKE MONEY

They say it takes money to make money, and that's actually true. The good news is that it doesn't take a *lot* of money.

What it does take is: (1) a regular source of income, or cash flow; (2) the discipline not to spend it all as soon as you get it; and (3) the ability to put whatever you keep for yourself to work. You begin by working for money and then money works for you. At some point, if you keep at it, you might discover that your money is working even harder—and eventually even earning more—than you are.

That's the fun stuff, and we'll get there soon. But right now, you need to give up any notion that there's a shortcut to the finish line. For almost all of us, building wealth is a slow, incremental, repetitive—not very exciting—process. The longer you do it, however, the easier it becomes and the more dramatic the results you're likely to see.

You will need a source of income (most likely a job) from which to save and spend. Making money work for you is the engine of your growth, but that income source is the fuel that makes it possible. Don't worry about how much you make or where you start your journey. Another person might make ten times what you do, but if the return on your investments is the same, you'll be building wealth just as rapidly relative to each of your incomes.

By the way, nothing is stopping you from *increasing* your income. That would allow you to save and invest even more. How do you increase what you're making? By becoming more valuable. By investing in yourself and constantly finding ways to add value to your employer or to the marketplace. By making yourself indispensable by doing jobs no one else wants to do. By improving the skills of your trade, especially if your employer will pay for the education and training. By starting a sideline business that doesn't require much, if any, start-up capital. Your boss expects and deserves your best efforts from nine to five, but what you do from five to nine is your business, and it will have everything to do with how financially successful you become, and how soon.

Remember, you can't expect your wealth to grow any faster than you do.

THE SECRET TO BUILDING WEALTH

Welcome to the most important concept in this book—one key idea. Right now, you are standing at a fork in the road to True Wealth. One way will help take you toward financial success, and the other could lead to difficulty and failure. *And it all depends on one simple idea* that is pivotal to your financial future.

None of the other ideas or strategies in this book will work unless you can follow one singular piece of advice. And if you absorb nothing more than this simple idea and *follow it consistently*, you will likely be better off financially than most people you will ever meet.

This idea could not be easier to understand. It is logical, reasonable, and intuitive. The risk is that you will be tempted to dismiss it as *too* simple or too obvious to have any real value. You'll miss it.

And if you already understand and agree with this advice but are not currently following it, ask yourself why. Why are you ignoring the most basic, fundamental principle of financial success? What's the key idea?

Spend less than you earn.

Stop spending money you haven't earned yet to buy things you don't need to impress people you don't even like.

Think about this: Over just a modest adult lifetime of work, it's likely that at least a million dollars will pass through your hands, and possibly several million. Very few people realize the enormous potential this income creates until it's too late. Most of those dollars will just slip through their fingers, never to be seen or enjoyed again.

Every dollar you earn gives you two simple choices: Keep it for yourself or give it to someone else. A dollar that you choose to spend today is a dollar that you can't spend in the future, but it's actually a lot more than that. At a hypothetical growth rate of 6% per year, net of inflation, every dollar you spend at age 25 is **$10** you won't be able to spend at age 65. Conversely, at the same rate of return, every dollar you *don't* spend at age 25 will be **$10** you *will* be able to spend when you're 65.

Put another way: **Wealth is what you choose not to spend.**

True Wealth means financial freedom, the ability to choose how to live. Every dollar you possess gives you the ability, the freedom, to control a tiny bit of the rest of your life. The more dollars you have, the more of your life you control.

> "Every dollar you save is like owning a slice of your future that might otherwise be managed by someone else, whatever their priorities are."
> —MORGAN HOUSEL

Remember our definition of True Wealth? It's when you no longer *have* to work for money. It's also when you are finally able to take full control of your future financial decisions. It's when you become financially free. And if you don't inherit it, win it, or marry into it, that freedom won't ever be yours unless you find a way to spend less than you earn from this day forward.

It will require figuring out what lifestyle you can afford today given your present income *and then consciously deciding to live on slightly less*, to earn a dollar and then decide to spend most but not all of it. Once you start doing that, something amazing will start to happen. That small difference between what you earn and what you spend will begin to accrue in your favor. It will make you a stronger, better person. Your self-confidence will begin to grow in step with your bank account.

Spending less than you earn isn't a one-time decision or a New Year's resolution. It's a habit that you alone must start and then maintain, like brushing your teeth. Once you're an adult, no one's going to be there looking over your shoulder making sure you do it. But you simply must, if you hope to succeed.

> "Smart people don't wait for luck to make them wealthy. Every day, they cultivate habits and follow rules that others don't. If you want to be wealthy, live below your means. Pay yourself first and build wealth, not a lifestyle that saddles you with expenses."
> —PAUL MERRIMAN

DIG YOUR MOAT

The Richest Man in Babylon is a book written in 1926 by George S. Clason. It won't take you long to read it, and it's well worth the time. It's a fictional story told in a series of parables about creating wealth. The first lesson is: "A part of all I earn is mine to keep."

When you spend less than you earn, the difference is yours to keep. And the trick to making sure that happens consistently is simply to *pay yourself before anyone else*. Then it simply becomes a matter of figuring out how to live on the rest of what you earn.

> "Do not save what is left after spending, but spend what is left over after saving."
> —WARREN BUFFETT

Your employer is legally required to withhold taxes from your paycheck because the IRS figured out a long time ago that it would be impossible for most taxpayers to pay what they owe each year all at one time. You probably pay income taxes, Social Security and Medicare taxes, and health insurance premiums automatically through regular payroll deductions, and it only makes sense that you should pay *yourself* in the same way.

So set up a new savings account—separate from the one you use to pay your bills—and start having a fixed amount of each paycheck automatically directed into it. The account should pay interest but be completely accessible to you if you need to withdraw from it at any time.

How much should go into it?

That depends on how important all of this is to you. If you really want to reach a point in life when you no longer have to work for money, I suggest you **pay yourself 15% of every dollar you earn (your gross income) from this day forward.**

Some people might suggest nibbling away at this goal to make it easier, starting perhaps with 5% and then increasing that amount by one per-cent or so every year. I don't subscribe to that idea, for two reasons. First, it delays your progress toward True Wealth. And, second, it requires you to make what could be a somewhat painful decision *over and over again*.

My advice: Do it once and do it now so you won't have to think about it anymore.

I will admit that saving 15% of your annual income might be the hardest thing you've ever asked yourself to do. It will certainly not be painless, especially if you haven't been saving anything at all up to now. But here's what I want to you realize: *You only have to act on this deci-sion once*, and after you've adjusted your lifestyle accordingly, things will get a lot easier. From that point forward, every time your income increases, the amount of money you're saving—and the amount you get to spend—will increase at the same rate as your income.

As you begin making these automatic savings deposits, think of it as digging a "moat" that one day will stand between you and unexpected financial setbacks, such as getting sick, losing your job, or getting hit with big, unexpected expenses. Your moat will certainly be narrow and shallow at first, but little by little, paycheck by paycheck, it will get deeper and wider. And eventually, it will be big enough to help protect you from all but the most serious financial setbacks. It won't make you rich, but it might very well keep you from ever being poor.

Your primary goal—before you do anything else with the money you're saving—is to build a financial reserve equal to **30% of your annual gross income**. If you earn $50,000 a year, that's $15,000. If your income is $250,000, your reserve should be $75,000. Your reserve should be relative to what you earn from your job and the lifestyle it's designed to protect.

If you don't currently have an emergency reserve—if your castle has no moat—saving 15% of your gross income annually will get you there in a little less than two years. In the next section, I will give you some ideas for getting there even faster. Right now, though, just focus on starting the habit of living on less than you earn and start watching your moat get deeper and wider with every savings deposit. Don't worry about anything else—not even paying off your credit cards or investing in your 401(k)—until you complete this essential goal.

Throughout the remainder of this book, I will be using the term *Reserve* to represent funds that you set aside for financial stability. Initially, it will help protect you in the event of financial emergencies. As you transition into True Wealth, this account will become a reservoir from which you will draw money to cover your spending needs once you stop working.

While the Reserve serves as the foundation of your lifelong plan, don't think of it as an investment. Investing is the fun part you get to do once your defenses are in place. Before you become a good investor, you must first become a good saver. It's not overly important what rate of return you earn on this emergency account, just that it remains stable and completely liquid in case you ever need to tap into it. If and when that day comes, you'll need to put everything else in your financial life on hold while you divert 100% of the money that you're saving from each paycheck back into it. Do this until your moat has been completely refilled and do your best to figure out how to prevent that emergency from happening again.

Some people will tell you that it's better to start saving in your employer's 401(k) plan or a similar retirement account, especially if your company matches part or all of your contribution. The match is free money, they argue, and it's foolish not to grab it. In addition, there are potentially tax advantages associated with saving for retirement.

That's well-meaning advice but ill-considered.

Why do I say that? Well, let's say you've been like many people, living paycheck to paycheck. What do you think will happen the next time you're faced with a financial emergency? With no savings to fall back on you'll probably have three choices:

1. Put the expense on your credit card and pay double-digit interest rates until it's paid off.

2. Withdraw the money from your 401(k) or similar retirement program, possibly triggering income taxes and early-withdrawal penalties, just to get access to your own money.

3. Borrow from the 401(k), which I believe is likely the best option of the three. At least the interest you pay goes back into your own account. But don't ignore the fact that the whole time the money stays outside of your 401(k), it's not working for you. And you might even miss out on that nice employer match.

The net result is that tapping retirement savings to cover a financial emergency could easily cost you more than you could have earned on it. In the process it might also break your savings habit and halt the magic of compounding, which we'll talk about shortly.

It's better to use retirement money for retirement, not for emergencies. Start digging that moat and shoring up your defenses. As they say in sports, offense wins games, but defense wins championships.

And full moats help keep financial dragons away from the door.

HOW TO MAKE YOURSELF SAVE

Years ago, I met a married couple who just couldn't find a way to save money. They got paid every Friday, went out to dinner on Saturday, paid bills on Sunday, and were broke again on Monday. They worked hard but had nothing to show for it.

Things changed dramatically for them one Friday when they didn't make it to the bank in time to cash their weekly paycheck. With no money in hand, there was no dinner out that weekend, no money to pay bills, and a mad dash to the bank on Monday morning to cash the prior week's paycheck.

And then they got a clever idea.

Having survived the weekend with no money to spend, and having stretched seven days of income over eight days of expenses, they decided to try it again. Only this time they waited until the following *Tuesday* to cash the check, and until *Wednesday* the week after that and so on until they successfully made it all the way to another Friday. At that point, the couple had not one but **two paychecks** in hand. They wisely decided to use the extra check to start a savings account and continue their little game.

One year later, this clever couple had received a total of 52 weekly paychecks but had spent only 44 of them. The eight "extra" checks had gone into their new savings account, equating to an annual savings rate of just over 15%. All from getting to the bank late one Friday and the creative thinking that it prompted.

That ingenious approach to saving money might not work as well in today's paperless, wireless world, but other ideas will. For example, two-income couples may decide to live on the larger paycheck and bank the other one. Or you may pick up some overtime hours or moonlight but not spend the extra income. Or squirrel away extra money received from bonuses, gifts, refunds, or proceeds from a garage sale, or use cash-back rewards from credit card purchases to build up your Reserve. Anything you can do to find and hold onto extra cash will help get your moat finished sooner. And those sacrifices need not be permanent.

Most of what you save, of course, will come from the habit of paying yourself 15% of your gross income, and the way to make your new savings habit easier is to make it *automatic*. Before long, you will have saved the equivalent of 30% of your annual income, and your moat will be full. From then on, you'll get to invest the money you save each month and make that money go to work for you like you worked for it.

Keep reminding yourself that *spending less than you earn* is the key to building wealth. And building wealth will be much easier once you're protected from unexpected expenses that would otherwise block your path.

The next step on your journey involves learning how to stop

spending money you haven't earned yet—and paying other people for the privilege.

WHY YOU SHOULD GET OUT OF DEBT

"Think what you do when you run in debt.
You give another power over your liberty."
—BENJAMIN FRANKLIN

It is hard to imagine surviving in today's world without debt. You can't book a flight, hotel, or rental car without a credit card. Student loans to pay the skyrocketing cost of a college education have become the norm. And without a mortgage, few of us would ever own a home.

Sometimes debt is simply necessary to build a life.

But loading up your credit cards to finance a lifestyle that you think will earn you the admiration and envy of others is, well, a very bad idea. And it's an idea that leads many otherwise intelligent people to financial ruin every day.

Ben Franklin knew that when you owe money, you are ceding control over a part of your life and your freedom to someone else—someone who probably doesn't care why you're a little short on the rent this month or can't make your car payment. All that matters to your creditors is that they get their money back—on time and with interest—before you find something else to spend it on.

Realize this: Until you understand how to control money—and harness its immense power to your benefit—money maintains the power to control *you*. Obtaining money through work and saving gives you options over how you live your life, now and in the future. Debt takes those options away.

What could you be doing now if you aren't burdened by debt? Looking for a nicer home? Starting a business on the side to generate extra income? Planning a nicer vacation? Providing a better life for your family?

Borrowing money so that you can spend more than you currently earn means less money that you will be able to spend in the future. It means you'll have to work longer and/or settle for a lower standard of living when you stop working, assuming you ever get to.

And if you carry substantial debt into retirement, it might force you to withdraw more from your retirement savings each year than you'd planned, which will mean paying higher income taxes. Higher taxable income could also mean you'll pay higher tax rates on your Social Security benefits and get charged larger Medicare premiums.

At its worst, excessive debt can put you into a box that you can't escape from without filing for bankruptcy. The added stress can ruin your marriage and shorten your life expectancy. Talk about giving up control over your life!

If you are over your head in debt right now, you probably haven't read anything here that you didn't already know. But you can overcome this situation. Once you learn how to make money work *for* you instead of *against* you, your life will start to get a little better and a little easier over time. The momentum will soon begin to shift, and money will become your ally. But only if you make it happen.

> "Imagine if I offered you an investment opportunity that had a guaranteed return of 15, 18, or even 22 percent. I suspect that, even if money were a little tight, you'd find a way to get in on the ground floor. And yet, if I told you that you could make the same amount of money by paying down your credit card debt, you'd probably find a number of excuses why that just isn't possible right now."
>
> **—CARL RICHARDS**

When we start talking about building wealth, I will give you some powerful examples of how money makes money, how it *compounds* itself over time. You've probably heard that when they asked Albert Einstein to name the greatest human invention in history, he reportedly answered, "compound interest." But a lot of people don't know the rest of his answer, which was even more enlightening: "He who understands it, earns it; he who doesn't, pays it."

Given enough time, compounding can turn the few dollars you save from every paycheck into millions. But compounding can also work against you. Debt compounds when you are charged interest on the money you borrow, which increases what you owe, which leads to even more interest being charged. Before long it gets difficult just making the interest payments, much less paying off your loan. Compounding debt destroys wealth, people, and even great societies.

The sooner you get money working for you instead of against you, the sooner you can reach True Wealth. If your goal is to reach a point in life where you no longer have to work for money, you will need to find a way to stop paying back money you spent but didn't earn, and all of the interest it has accrued in the meantime.

As I've said, your first financial goal is to create a Reserve equivalent to 30% of your annual gross income. Your next priority should be to eliminate all of your nonmortgage debt. It is completely possible to do them both at the same time, and it's time for you to learn how.

HOW TO GET OUT OF DEBT

I'm about to give you a seven-step plan designed to eliminate all of your nonmortgage debt. Once that's gone, you will have the luxury of paying off your mortgage as well if you choose. Ideally, you should be *completely* debt free by the time you stop working, but unless current interest rates are sky high, you will probably find more productive uses for your money than getting ahead on your house payments.

I've already pointed out that paying 15% of your gross income to yourself—before you pay anyone else—is the key to building wealth. Simultaneously paying down your debt allows you to pursue this goal from both directions.

In accounting terms, *assets* represent what you *own*, and *liabilities* are what you *owe*. The difference between the two is your *net worth*, or wealth. When you save money, you increase your assets, and when you pay down debt, you decrease your liabilities. Both are essential to building wealth, and if you do them at the same time your net worth will grow even faster.

If that idea appeals to you, **start setting aside another 5% of your gross income to pay down your debt.**

Saving 15% while putting another 5% toward your debts adds up to 20% of your gross income off the top. That leaves 80% of your income to pay taxes and live the best lifestyle you can afford. Again, this will almost certainly be a challenge at first, but you will be able to adapt. Have you ever heard people complain that they're barely scraping by on what they earn, but then they get a big raise or a better-paying job, and six months later they're somehow just scraping by again?

That's called *lifestyle creep*. The amount of money we "need" to support our lifestyle always seems to expand automatically in step with our income, and before we know it, there's "too much month left at the end of the money" all over again. But with some ingenuity and effort, you can find ways to spend less than you do now without dramatically lowering your standard of living. There are some relatively painless ways to live on less, but for now let's focus on getting your debt under control.

As you implement the plan that follows, it's important that you have some way to track your progress. Create a spreadsheet, find an app, or buy a journal or notebook to record the information below. You need to be able to know—to the penny—what you're up against, and, just as importantly, to see the progress you'll be making once you implement this seven-step debt-elimination plan.

Step 1: Stop borrowing. Commit to stop taking on new debts until you bring your situation under control. Put the credit cards away for a while and start managing your day-to-day spending on a cash basis as much as possible. Make purchases with cash, check, debit card, or by electronic draft—nothing that will lead to new finance charges.

Step 2: Have minimum payments on each of your debts automatically deducted from your bank account each month. This is the same principle we are using to *save* money from every paycheck, and the more automatic the process, the easier it will be and the less chance you'll have of breaking the habit. Here's a crucial point: Your minimum payments should come out of the 80% of the income you get to spend each month. We want to apply all of the extra 5% you're saving to paying down your credit balances, not to cover new spending.

Step 3: Make a detailed list of all of your debts. For each debt, record the name of the lender, the annual percentage rate (APR) of interest you're being charged, the outstanding balance, and the current minimum monthly payment. Mortgage debt should automatically go at the bottom of your list.

Once you've listed all your debts, rank them by the interest rate each charges. Some people recommend that you pay off your smallest accounts first, to give yourself a psychological boost and some momentum. But if you want to pay off your debts more quickly and efficiently, pay off the debt with the *highest* interest rate first. Both strategies can work, so just decide which one seems better for you and commit to it.

Step 4: Calculate your debt-to-income ratio (DTI) and record it. If you have a debt problem, this number will tell you the extent of it. Soon, it will also show you the progress you're making toward overcoming it.

Here's how to calculate your DTI:

1. Add up your *total monthly required debt payments*: mortgage, consumer loans, car payments, credit card minimum payments, etc. Now you can see exactly what it costs each month to service your debt.

2. Divide this number by your *gross monthly income.*

3. The result is your current *debt-to-income ratio,* or DTI.

4. Multiply this number by 100 to convert it to a *percentage.*

Let's say your gross income is currently $90,000 per year, or $7,500 per month. When you add up your mortgage and car payments, the minimum payments on your credit cards, and student loans, plus any other debt-related payments due each month, it totals $3,375. Dividing your debt-service amount ($3,375) by your monthly gross income ($7,500) gets you a debt-to-income ratio of 0.45, or 45%.

What's an acceptable debt-to-income ratio? To qualify for most mortgages, it should be less than 43%. A DTI below 36% is preferable, however, with mortgage payments accounting for no more than 28% of the total.

Of course, once all your debts are paid off in full, the ratio will be a big, fat zero. That's what we're aiming for.

Step 5: Consider a balance-transfer credit card. There are promotional offers that allow you—if you qualify—to move one or more of your high-interest credit card balances onto a new card with a low introductory rate, sometimes zero. The credit card company will likely charge a fee for each balance you transfer, which gets added to what you owe.

These low promotional rates are often good for only six to 12 months, but that will buy you some time to make big progress toward paying off your credit card debt and give you a nice head start and some breathing room. During the time the interest rate remains low, all or most of your monthly payments will go toward paying down principal, which will bring down your balance even faster.

Don't play games with this, however. Moving balances around from one credit card to another won't help your credit score, especially if you try to do it more than once. One thing that *will* help your score eventually is getting out of debt, and this strategy could help if used properly.

Step 6: Pick your number-one target. Once you decide which debt you want to eliminate first, apply the full 5% portion of your income to it. Keep making the minimum payments on all other debts from the rest of your monthly income and apply all of this *extra* money to your number-one target until it's completely gone.

Step 7: Move right to the next one. When the debt balance on your first target is reduced to zero, move to the next one on your list. Put 5% of your gross income toward it until it's extinguished, and then keep repeating this momentum-building process until all of your nonmortgage debts are paid in full.

As you progress on this plan, you'll start to see something really nice taking place. As each debt is paid down, its required monthly payments will also decrease. And because those minimum payments have been coming from the 80% of your income that you use for spending, you will be able gradually to spend more on the things you need and want.

And as your debts are paid off one by one, you'll see your efforts begin to snowball. You are learning to make money work *for* you instead of *against* you—and it will feel absolutely wonderful.

NOW YOU'VE GOT OPTIONS

Getting debt under control can take some time, but you will have taken the first giant steps toward True Wealth, first by setting up a savings program and building your Reserve, and second by launching a strategy to pay off your nonmortgage debt.

Once those debts are behind you—never to be seen or heard from again—you will no longer need to set aside 5% of your income to pay back your creditors. And you will have at least four choices on what to do with that money, all of them very attractive.

First, you could redirect the 5% toward your mortgage if you have one. Paying it off early could save you tens of thousands of dollars in future interest charges while building equity in your home, another way to build wealth. That's never a bad idea, especially if mortgage rates are high, but as I mentioned before, you might have other goals that are more important to you at present.

Second, if you don't own a home yet but want to, you can use the 5% to save for a down payment. The more money you put down, the lower your monthly payments, and a larger down payment might also help you avoid having to purchase private mortgage insurance (PMI), which lenders often require.

Third, if real estate isn't in your plans, you could use the extra cash flow to start funding a college savings plan for your children, pay cash for your next car, take the big trip you've always dreamed of, or save up for a big purchase. You get the idea: This 5% of your income can pay for nice things you might have been going into debt for up until now.

Finally, you might decide just to add this 5% back to the 80% of your income that you've been spending to support your lifestyle. That should certainly make your life a bit easier, which is something you'll deserve once you've dug yourself out of a debt problem.

Whether it takes months or years to get your nonmortgage debt behind you, it's absolutely essential that you do these three things to help keep it there:

1. Consider every purchase you make with a credit card from now on to be part of the 85% of your income that you get to spend. It's an expense, a bill to pay now instead of later, so treat it that way.

2. Pay off your credit balances in full each month. No more balances carried over. No more buy now/pay later. No more finance charges.

3. Recalculate your debt-to-income ratio at least once a year and keep a written record of it. Compare it with the mileposts at the end of this book.

You might have been wondering all this time why you shouldn't just focus on paying off all of your debts *before* starting a savings program, especially if interest rates are higher than what you're likely to earn from saving and investing. After all, isn't paying off a 14% credit card essentially the same as earning 14% on an investment?

Yes, it is, and that's a fair question. However, the more you save— *and the sooner you start*—the more distance you are putting between yourself and your next financial setback, and the less likely you'll have to borrow your way out of it.

The sooner you save, the more you are putting time on your side, which is the key to compounding. That means every day you delay getting started is *at least* one day longer you will have to wait for True Wealth, and the longer you wait, the harder it will be for you.

Saving money and reducing debt are equally powerful ways to build wealth—and important enough to do them both at the same time.

FOCUS ON HOW YOU SPEND

Having an important job with a nice income might be a very good thing, but contrary to popular belief it won't necessarily make you wealthy. In fact, by the time all is said and done, how much money you *make* isn't nearly as important as how you *spend* it.

If you've been following my advice so far, you're now paying out the first 15% of your gross income to yourself, or to be exact, for your *future*. And if you have any nonmortgage debt, you're spending the next 5% of your income paying off your creditors. In essence, you're paying back money you spent in the *past* before you earned it.

Now, it's time to focus on the *present*: how to live the best life possible with the 80% or 85% of your gross income that remains. We have already acknowledged that this will not be the easiest thing you've ever done, but it's far from impossible. I'm willing to bet that there are thousands if not millions of people living in the same country as you right now who are already enjoying a pretty decent life on 80% or less of what you currently earn. And regardless of your current income, you can do it, too.

> "When your outgo exceeds your income,
> your upkeep becomes your downfall."
> —JIM ROHN

The trick to living on less is first to find out exactly where your money is going, and then discovering the least painful ways to reduce your expenses. The task will be easier if you break your spending down into categories and begin working on them one at a time. First, let's focus on determining how you are currently spending each precious dollar that comes your way.

Start immediately by getting yourself a notebook and writing down what you spend each day. *Every single thing you spend.* From the coffee drink you buy on the way to work to the mortgage payment you make by the end every month. If you purchase something with a credit or debit card, log it in your notebook. If bills are getting paid out of your bank account automatically, subscriptions for example, make a note of them as they happen. If you drop a quarter in a tip jar, write it down.

You can keep this exercise in an analog form or go digital. There are dozens of financial apps that will help you track your spending, even sorting it into categories for you, which might come in handy soon. For now, the important thing is getting into the habit of recording every expense, not which method you use. The very idea that you are now paying close attention every time you spend money will go a long way toward helping you eventually control it.

Follow this habit faithfully for the next 90 days, and you'll start to see some patterns develop. You will discover where most of your money has been going. You'll start to question some of the things you're paying for and whether they are worth it. And you'll begin getting ideas on where you might be able to spend less without sacrificing your lifestyle.

At the end of 90 days, you will be ready to make some improvements.

You'll not only be able to live on less, but you might be able to live even better.

SPENDING CATEGORIES

If you've bought in to the full saving habit—paying yourself 15% of everything you earn and applying another 5% to your nonmortgage debts—you're probably feeling some stress about how to make ends meet with what is left over. Help is on the way.

Make sure you understand the math behind all of this: For every dollar you earn, you are paying yourself 15 cents; you are saving that money, increasing your assets, and building equity in yourself. If you have debts other than a mortgage, another nickel of every dollar goes to your creditors, which is shrinking your liabilities and helping boost your net worth. That leaves 80 or 85 cents of every dollar you earn for you to live on.

Before you ever see that money, however, the tax man takes his share of your earnings through payroll deductions. Your job will be figuring out how to live the best life you can after you've paid yourself, your creditors, and the government.

Here's the formula:

Gross Income **minus** *Taxes* **minus**
Savings **minus** *Debt Reduction* = *Spending*

Get a handle on that net spending number. Write it down at the top of a piece of paper. That's the money you have allocated yourself to live on each month, and to get the most from it, break it down into spending *categories*. We are going to focus on one category at a time, looking for ways to spend less in each one.

Use your 90-day spending journal to see what you've been spending in each category and to compare your findings with the general guidelines below. Then work your way through the list, one category at a time, looking for opportunities to live just as well or even better on less.

HOUSING: 30% OF SPENDING. The typical consumer spends more on housing than any other category. That means any savings you find here will likely have the greatest impact on your overall spending. Housing includes your monthly mortgage or rent payments, property taxes, homeowners/renters insurance costs, repairs and improvements, neighborhood association dues, and housekeeping services.

Ways to reduce housing costs:

1. Move to a smaller, less expensive home.

2. Sell your home and rent something cheaper if it makes economic sense.

3. Refinance your mortgage.

4. Bundle your homeowners/renters insurance coverage with other policies (auto, liability, etc.) with the same company to get discounts. Shop other insurers periodically for a better deal.

5. Challenge your property-tax assessment if it seems out of line with where you live, especially if it has recently been increased.

6. Clean and perform simple housing repairs and maintenance yourself.

TRANSPORTATION: 20% OF SPENDING. It's normal to spend up to half of your disposable income on just having a place to live and a way to get around. Transportation costs include loan or lease payments, fuel, repairs and maintenance, auto insurance, ride-sharing expenses, parking, tolls, and public-transportation fares.

Ways to reduce transportation costs:

1. Commute or carpool to your work, or work from home if it's an option.

2. Shop for less expensive gasoline. Check online tracking services for your area or consider joining a warehouse club to get better prices.

3. If your family owns more than one vehicle, see if it's feasible to get rid of one, at least until your spending is under control.

4. Keep your current car longer before trading it in, but be sure to keep up with repairs and scheduled maintenance.

5. Before you buy your next car, research the best time of year and day of the week to make your purchase. Know the dealer's cost and learn to negotiate. And keep your focus on the cost of the car, not the size of the monthly payments.

FOOD: 15% OF SPENDING. Pretty simple definition here: everything you and your family eat or drink goes into this category. That includes groceries, meals at restaurants, fast food, pizza deliveries, ice cream runs, vending machines, pet food, and so on.

Ways to reduce food costs:

1. Stop buying bottled water. It's expensive, generally bad for the environment, and most of the time completely unnecessary. And walking around with a name-brand bottle of water doesn't even make you look cool anymore.

2. Add up how many meals you eat at restaurants each month and reduce it by one. Explore new places to eat by using coupons and advertised offers. Limit ordering alcohol when you eat out.

3. Learn how to cook. It will save money, improve your health, and possibly develop into an enjoyable hobby. Plan your meals in advance and build your plan around what's on sale each week. Save time, energy, and money by preparing several meals at once.

4. At the supermarket, shop sales, use coupons on the brands you use, and try out generics and store brands. Buy in bulk when it makes sense.

5. Avoid vending machines.

We've now covered the big three categories, which can easily account for two-thirds of your monthly spending. Now let's zero in on the smaller areas for more savings opportunities:

UTILITIES: 10% OF SPENDING. Utilities include gas, electric, water, sewer, garbage, home security, internet, and cell phone services. You have much more control over this category than you might assume.

Ways to reduce utility costs:

1. Once a year, reevaluate how you use your cell phone. Consider changing your plan or even switching carriers. Sign up for family discounts. Upgrade your phone less frequently. Get rid of paid apps and subscriptions you can do without.

2. Bundle your utility contracts (internet, phone, home security) where possible, and negotiate every few years for lower rates.

3. See if your electric utility offers free home energy audits and schedule one.

4. Install a programmable thermostat and learn how to use it to make heating and cooling your home more efficient and less expensive.

5. Replace furnace/AC filters on a regular schedule. Use ceiling fans more often. Switch to energy-efficient appliances and light bulbs. Turn off electronics when you're not using them.

HEALTH CARE: 10% OF SPENDING. This category includes health insurance premiums, deductibles, co-payments, prescriptions, and doctor and dentist bills. Don't cut corners here, but make sure you're getting what you pay for.

Ways to reduce health-care costs:

1. Work on your health; stop smoking, eat less, and eat better to improve your health and save money. Exercise more (which might also lower transportation costs).

2. Become an expert on your health-care benefits. Know what expenses you are required to cover out-of-pocket, and schedule elective procedures and visits around your coverage.

3. Sign up for a health savings account (HSA) or flexible-spending account (FSA) at work; these can have special tax benefits. Take advantage of any free health-related programs your employer offers.

4. Review every medical bill you receive and try to negotiate payments for big expenses that aren't covered by your insurance.

5. Other ideas: Ask about generic prescription drugs, avoid the ER for nonemergencies, ask questions about the need for expensive tests, and develop a good working relationship with your primary care physician.

PERSONAL/RECREATION: 10% OF SPENDING.
This category includes vacations, travel expenses, memberships, concert tickets, haircuts, admissions, club dues, hobbies, subscriptions, postage, tobacco, alcohol, and other forms of entertainment.

Ways to reduce personal/recreation costs:

1. Get a library card and open yourself up to a world of books, magazines, movies, classes, lectures, and online resources—*all for free.*

2. Plan vacations and trips carefully. Limit your travel to destinations you can reach by car, at least for the time being. Look for travel deals from organizations you belong to, such as AAA, other clubs, and alumni associations.

3. Decide how much time you want to devote to watching TV every month and think seriously about what you are paying for it. Get rid of any service you're not watching unless it's tied to something you do plan to watch.

4. Attend low-cost events with friends, such as amateur sports, community theater, and local museums.

5. And never buy another lottery ticket for as long as you live. Wealthy people don't play the lottery, and it's not because they don't need to. *Nobody needs to*—especially people with money troubles.

CLOTHING: 5% OF SPENDING. This category covers everything you wear and how you care for it, including laundry, dry cleaning, repairs, and alterations.

Ways to reduce clothing costs:

1. Build a basic wardrobe of clothing essentials. Buy quality but skip fashion labels. Learn to mix and match outfits. Expand your options with accessories.

2. Shop out of season. Retailers sell clothing one season ahead and mark up prices accordingly. You'll often find the best deals late in the current season, even if you have to wait until next year to wear them.

3. Look for deals. Clothing is one of the most heavily discounted areas of retail. Shop sales, use coupons, sign up for rewards programs, and take those surveys on the back of your receipts if they translate into immediate economic benefits.

4. Steer clear of flashy displays in the center of the store. Many clothing retailers are known to keep their best bargains and sale items toward the back or around the edges of the store.

5. Keep your clothes clean and store them with care. Avoid clothes with a "dry-clean-only" tag whenever possible. Before washing anything with a zipper, zip it up to prevent the teeth from ripping other garments in the washer or dryer. Wash your clothes in cold water with a less expensive detergent in a high-efficiency washer. Dry them on a clothesline when possible.

TAKEAWAYS:
A FEW FINAL POINTS
BEFORE WE MOVE ON:

- You should adjust the above percentages to your own life-style and spending habits.

- Money you don't spend in one category can be shifted to the others.

- Focus on your biggest expenses first for the greatest impact.

- Keep looking for ways to plug "cash leaks" as you spot them and stay disciplined when it comes to new purchases.

- Always buy the best quality you can afford when it matters—especially for nondisposables like cars and clothes—even when it costs a little more. And then hang onto them for as long as you can.

CHAPTER 5

BUILDING WEALTH BY INVESTING

L et's pause for a second and take some measure of what you're doing for yourself.

You have begun to build some financial habits that will serve you well for the rest of your life. And those habits will start paying you dividends soon if they haven't already. Even if you can't see them yet, know that those benefits are starting to accrue.

It's important to give these new habits time to work. Keep taking little steps, day after day, paycheck after paycheck. Make those automatic savings deposits. Whittle down your debts, one at a time. Find one new idea each day to get more from each dollar you spend. Feed your brain and get a little smarter every week to increase your value in the workplace. Finish reading and studying this book.

You have also learned how to pay yourself the first portion of all the income you earn, and you will soon put these dollars to work making more dollars for you. As you earn money, whatever you save will also start earning money on its own. One day, you might even reach the point where your savings are earning more than you are. On that wonderful day, you will realize that your money has been working so hard for you that you no longer need to work for it.

FROM SAVER TO INVESTOR

It's now time to transition your thinking from saver to investor, and that's what the next few chapters of this book are all about. It might take you more time to finish your moat if you haven't already, but you'll want to be ready to start investing as soon as you do. You should not wait until you're free of nonmortgage debt to begin investing, especially if your debt is substantial. Save and invest while you're paying off debts. That's how to build wealth.

Almost immediately, you'll see the asset side of your ledger start to grow. This money belongs to you now because *you earned it*. It's the first spadeful of dirt, a tiny hole in the ground that will one day be your moat, a financial reserve that will help protect you from future setbacks. When your Reserve is full, you won't have to go into debt for every little emergency or unexpected expense. The interest you would have otherwise paid to someone else will instead keep working for you.

Take good care of that Reserve. It will be with you for the rest of your life.

Now consider the liability side of your ledger. As you follow your debt-reduction plan, the amount of money working *against* you will start to shrink. Here, too, your progress might be hard to detect right away, but keep at it and one by one you'll see those credit balances shrink and disappear. Over time your debt-to-income ratio will get lower, and your credit score will likely improve, which has its own potential benefits.

I hope by now you are also finding ways to enjoy life on the remaining

80% or 85% of your income. You're starting to think creatively about how you spend. And perhaps in your spare time you have discovered low-cost ways to invest in yourself and your skills to increase your earning power, which in turn could give you even more resources to apply toward your goal of achieving True Wealth.

The net result of this is that your financial life will get simpler, easier, and less stressful if it hasn't already. Each step you take toward True Wealth will make you feel better about your future—and better about yourself.

ONE EXTRA DOLLAR

Benjamin Franklin probably had the simplest explanation of compounding when he said: "Money makes money. And the money that money makes, makes money." That should be an easy concept to grasp, but a simple illustration will reveal the immense power in his statement.

Let's say you have $100 to invest and you're able to earn a hypothetical 10% return on it in a year's time. A year from now, you'll have $110. And assuming your annual investment return remains 10%, you'll keep collecting $10 bills every year for as long as you want. After 30 years, you'll still have your original $100 investment, plus another $300 in interest, for a total of $400. We refer to this concept as "simple" interest.

But what would happen if you were also able to put those interest payments to work along with your principal each year? In Franklin's words, your $100 makes money: $10 per year. And then the money that your *money* makes—that $10—can also make money every year from now on. We call that "compound" interest.

Here's how our hypothetical illustration would play out over 30 years:

| Year | Simple interest on $100 | | Compound interest on $100 | | Annual |
	Interest	Total	Interest	Total	Difference
1	$10	$110	$10	$110	$0
2	$10	$120	$11	$121	$1
3	$10	$130	$12	$133	$2
4	$10	$140	$13	$146	$3
5	$10	$150	$15	$161	$5
6	$10	$160	$16	$177	$6
7	$10	$170	$18	$195	$8
8	$10	$180	$19	$214	$9
9	$10	$190	$21	$236	$11
10	$10	$200	$24	$259	$14
11	$10	$210	$26	$285	$16
12	$10	$220	$29	$314	$19
13	$10	$230	$31	$345	$21
14	$10	$240	$35	$380	$25
15	$10	$250	$38	$418	$28
16	$10	$260	$42	$459	$32
17	$10	$270	$46	$505	$36
18	$10	$280	$51	$556	$41
19	$10	$290	$56	$612	$46
20	$10	$300	$61	$673	$51
21	$10	$310	$67	$740	$57
22	$10	$320	$74	$814	$64
23	$10	$330	$81	$895	$71
24	$10	$340	$90	$985	$80
25	$10	$350	$98	$1,083	$88
26	$10	$360	$108	$1,192	$98
27	$10	$370	$119	$1,311	$109
28	$10	$380	$131	$1,442	$121
29	$10	$390	$144	$1,586	$134
30	$10	$400	$159	$1,745	$149

This chart is for illustration purposes only. Actual investor results will vary.

Take a look at the first line: Year 1. Assuming you receive your interest payment at the end of each year, you'll have the same amount of money under both methods: $110. The magic of compounding begins in the *second* year, when the $10 interest earned in Year 1 is reinvested. At a 10% hypothetical return, that $10 interest payment will earn another $1 on its own. And that *one extra dollar* represents the difference between simple and compound returns at the end of Year 2.

One extra dollar might not seem like a big deal, but it's a dollar you didn't have before. It's a dollar you didn't have to work for. And it's another dollar that will get put to work for you in Year 3 and *every* year thereafter.

Something else you will notice about compounding: Even with an attractive hypothetical return of 10% a year, it takes a long time to really work. In the above illustration, there was only a $1 difference after Year 2, and only a $14 difference after Year 10. In fact, after 10 full years of watching your money grow, your $100 investment has compounded to $259, versus $200 under the simple-interest method. That doesn't seem like a huge advantage over a decade, but let's keep going.

By the end of Year 19, notice that you would have accumulated *twice* as much from compounding as from simple interest. By the end of Year 25, *three times* as much. And at the end of 30 years, your $100 initial investment would be worth more than *four times* as much due to compounding: $1,745 versus $400. All because of compounding, all because of time.

> "Compounding is the magic of investing."
> **—JIM ROGERS**

Compounding requires three ingredients, and the first of them is *money*. As we discussed earlier, it does take money to make money, because compounding zero dollars at 10% (or any other rate of return) gets you . . . exactly zero dollars. But now that you are paying *yourself* something every payday, finding money to invest isn't an obstacle for you any longer. And once your moat is deep and wide enough, you can really unleash the power of compounding as you transition from saver to investor.

The second ingredient of compounding is the *return* you earn on the money you have saved and invested, and we will get into that shortly.

The third and final ingredient of compounding—the most powerful one—is *time*. Your next-door neighbor might be paid a higher salary than you, and your sister-in-law might earn 1% more than you on her portfolio next year, but both pale in comparison to the importance of time when it comes to making money compound. And the younger you are, the greater advantage time gives you, regardless of how much you have to invest.

THERE ARE NO SHORTCUTS

Early in life, most of us have a lot more time than money. Later in life, it's typically the opposite. It's a fortunate soul who discovers and heeds life's lessons while there's still ample time to profit from them.

Imagine two young friends, both age 22 and earning identical incomes, each with the same opportunities to save and invest the same amount of money every year. At the end of the first year, Investor A decides to deposit $5,000 into a hypothetical investment that earns 8% annually. Investor B, on the other hand, chooses to postpone investing for the time being.

This same thing happens every year for a decade. After 10 years, both are age 32. Investor A has now contributed a total of $50,000 into his fund, which—through annual compounding at 8%—has grown in value to $72,433. But now, for whatever reason, Investor A decides to *stop* adding to his fund and will simply leave it invested to grow without any further contributions.

Seeing the success his friend has enjoyed, Investor B decides to *begin* investing the identical $5,000 at the end of each year in the same hypo-thetical fund, earning the same hypothetical 8% return each year. He commits to doing this for as long as it takes to catch up with his friend, Investor A.

Now fast-forward to our friends at age 65 and see how this turns out. Investor A, who invested a total of **$50,000** over the first **10 years** of this exercise—and nothing at all thereafter, now has **$991,615.**

Investor B, who put off investing anything for the first 10 years, then invested a total of **$170,000** over the following **34 years**—more than *three times* as much as his friend—has **$793,133.**

The difference between these two final sums—nearly $200,000—illustrates both the power of time and the cost of waiting to invest. Both investors are the same age, with the same amount of money to invest and the same number of years ahead of them. They earned identical investment returns each year, but Investor B never did catch up with Investor A, and in fact he never will. That's why we say the true secret of compounding has little to do with money and every-thing to do with *time*.

	Investor A			Investor B		
Age	Saves	Earns	Year-end	Saves	Earns	Year-end
22	$5,000	$0	$5,000	$0	$0	$0
23	$5,000	$400	$10,400	$0	$0	$0
24	$5,000	$832	$16,232	$0	$0	$0
25	$5,000	$1,299	$22,531	$0	$0	$0
26	$5,000	$1,802	$29,333	$0	$0	$0
27	$5,000	$2,347	$36,680	$0	$0	$0
28	$5,000	$2,934	$44,614	$0	$0	$0
29	$5,000	$3,569	$53,183	$0	$0	$0
30	$5,000	$4,255	$62,438	$0	$0	$0
31	$5,000	$4,995	$72,433	$0	$0	$0
32	$0	$5,795	$78,227	$5,000	$0	$5,000
33	$0	$6,258	$84,486	$5,000	$400	$10,400
34	$0	$6,759	$91,244	$5,000	$832	$16,232
35	$0	$7,300	$98,544	$5,000	$1,299	$22,531
36	$0	$7,884	$106,428	$5,000	$1,802	$29,333
37	$0	$8,514	$114,942	$5,000	$2,347	$36,680
38	$0	$9,195	$124,137	$5,000	$2,934	$44,614
39	$0	$9,931	$134,068	$5,000	$3,569	$53,183
40	$0	$10,725	$144,794	$5,000	$4,255	$62,438
41	$0	$11,583	$156,377	$5,000	$4,995	$72,433
42	$0	$12,510	$168,887	$5,000	$5,795	$83,227
43	$0	$13,511	$182,398	$5,000	$6,258	$94,886
44	$0	$14,591	$196,990	$5,000	$6,759	$107,476
45	$0	$15,759	$212,749	$5,000	$7,300	$121,075
50	$0	$23,155	$312,598	$5,000	$14,980	$207,231
55	$0	$34,023	$459,310	$5,000	$24,357	$333,824
60	$0	$49,991	$674,876	$5,000	$38,136	$519,830
65	$0	$73,453	$991,615	$5,000	$58,380	$793,133
44 years	$50,000	$941,615	$991,615	$170,000	$623,133	$793,133

This chart is for illustration purposes only. Actual investor results will vary.

It's clear that building wealth takes time and patience. If you're looking for instant gratification, you will be disappointed. The benefits of compounding are incremental and cumulative: The longer you keep at it, the bigger results you are likely to eventually see. In the meantime, you cannot afford to be impatient or discouraged.

And don't make the mistake of thinking that compounding requires big investment returns to work its magic. Above-average returns don't seem to happen very often and are less likely to be sustainable for the long run. A modest rate of return, repeated over time, is more likely to give you the results you need. Just build your compounding machine, feed it regularly, reinvest the returns you receive, and give the magic time to work.

Finally, don't waste precious time looking for shortcuts. The most successful investors will tell you there aren't any. If you lose patience with the process, you'll start making bad decisions, which become bad strategies, which lead to bad results. That might be enough to cause you to give up along the way, and you simply can't afford to do that.

The key to building wealth is a simple process. There is no secret formula, shortcut, or undiscovered truth.

> "Truth is ever to be found in simplicity, and not in the multiplicity of things."
> **—ISAAC NEWTON**

Any great artist, performer, writer, surgeon, athlete, artisan, or investor will probably admit that their genius doesn't come from doing incredible things that other people are not able to do. It comes when they learn the simple yet essential requirements of their craft, then master them completely. In a similar way, building wealth comes from first learning what to do and then doing it over and over again.

You can do that. You already are.

WHERE TO BEGIN INVESTING

Until you have accumulated a reserve equal to 30% of your annual gross income, there is no other place you should be saving money. Saving 15% of your gross income for two years will get you there, sooner if you already have some liquid savings put away or find some extra cash somewhere. Once your Reserve is full, however, you will need to decide where to direct your future savings deposits.

Here are some ideas for prioritizing your investment choices. You probably can't do them all, so start at the top and work your way down the list as your income increases over time.

PRIORITY #1: Workplace retirement plan

If your employer offers a 401(k) or similar retirement plan, start there. These accounts typically allow your savings to grow tax deferred until you need them in retirement, and if the company will match any part of your contribution, so much the better. An employer match amounts to free money, and you cannot afford to turn it down. Even if your employer matches only one dollar for every 10 that you contribute, that's an automatic 10% return on your investment, and you'll have trouble doing better than that anywhere else. Many employers are more generous with their matching percentages, giving you an even greater incentive to participate.

PRIORITY #2: Roth IRA

If you don't have a retirement savings plan at work—or if your employer doesn't offer matching contributions—open a Roth IRA and fund it up to the annual contribution limit. There is no up-front tax advantage to a Roth, but, once invested, your money can grow and compound on a tax-deferred basis. If and when you withdraw money from your Roth IRA—once certain conditions are met—it's all tax free to you. And unlike traditional IRAs, Roth IRAs don't require you to make minimum annual withdrawals once you reach a certain age. (Contribution limits and income restrictions may have changed by the time you read this, so do some research on the current requirements.)

PRIORITY #3: Back to the company plan

Once you have funded your Roth IRA to the max each year, go back to your 401(k) or similar retirement plan and resume contributions until you reach the annual limit. Even without a match, these dollars can grow on a tax-deferred basis, and there may be other benefits to you as well. If your employer's plan offers a Roth option, it's an option worth considering, but I like the idea of fully funding a Roth IRA if you're eligible before returning to the company plan. IRAs offer a much broader array of investment options and potentially lower costs.

PRIORITY #4: Traditional IRA

If you take full advantage of the employer match *and* fully fund your Roth IRA *and* hit the maximum contribution limits on your employer plan *and* still have money to invest toward your goal of True Wealth . . . *Nice job!* Above certain income levels, however, you might not be *allowed* to contribute to a Roth IRA. In that case, fund a traditional IRA instead, even if your contributions are not tax deductible. Your funds will still be able to grow on a tax-deferred basis until you begin taking distributions, at which point they are generally taxable as ordinary income. Your after-tax, nondeductible contributions will eventually come back to you tax free as a portion of each future distribution.

PRIORITY #5: Health Savings Account (HSA)

At this writing, health savings accounts offer the potential of triple-tax advantages under certain conditions. Contributions are made with pretax dollars, compounding is tax deferred, and distributions for qualifying health-related expenses are tax free. HSAs can be a valuable supplement to traditional savings plans and an additional source of retirement income if you choose to leave the money alone until you stop working.

PRIORITY #6: After-tax investment accounts

Clearly, it makes sense to save for the future in tax-deferred or tax-free accounts, and you should take full advantage of these opportunities where they exist. Beyond that, however, there is nothing stopping you from continuing to save and invest as much as you want on an *after-tax* basis. This could be a mutual fund, non-IRA brokerage account or any other investment vehicle that's not tax deferred. Depending on how investment income and capital gains are taxed under current law, it might even be possible to reduce and/or defer some of the taxes for some of the investments you make in these accounts. At the very least, having money invested in all three ways—tax-free, tax-deferred, and after-tax—will give you some welcome flexibility when it comes time to withdraw money for retirement expenses.

Remember that tax laws might have changed significantly since this book was published. The full tax implications of these savings priorities are beyond its scope. I encourage you to thoroughly research each of the above options—and any more that may have been created—before you begin investing. And consult a qualified tax advisor to help you put together an appropriate strategy.

DONORS, LOANERS, AND OWNERS

If you are familiar with sports, chess, or military conquests, you understand the concept of "offense" and "defense." They are two different strategies with opposing objectives, yet both pursue a common goal. Offense helps you win the game, match, or battle. Defense helps you avoid losing it.

And so it is with investing. Why do castles have moats? To protect and *defend* their inhabitants. And why is building the Reserve the first step toward building wealth? To help protect and *defend* ourselves against financial threats. Without a solid defense in place, we might never get to play offense. To win, one must first survive.

Certain investment vehicles are defensive by nature. Their prices are relatively stable, their returns consistent and predictable, and principal values are often secured by legal promises or guarantees from the issuer.

By contrast, offense-oriented investments seldom come with such assurances. Their prices typically fluctuate unpredictably—at least over the short term—and while they often have the potential to appreciate in value over the long term, that's never guaranteed.

Think of it this way. With every dollar you earn, you have three choices. You can be a "donor," a "loaner," or an "owner." When you *spend* that dollar, you "donate" it to someone else in exchange for whatever goods and services you receive in return for it. It might be a necessary purchase or a complete waste of money, but either way, your dollar is gone. It is now owned and working for someone other than you.

Alternatively, you could decide to *lend* your dollar to someone else. As a loaner, you typically exchange your money for a promise that you'll get it back on some specified date in the future, along with a fixed rate of return (interest) paid to you by the borrower in the interim.

Finally, as an owner you exchange your dollar for an ownership stake in a business enterprise. Your investment then becomes tied to the success or failure of that particular undertaking. If the venture succeeds, your ownership stake stands to increase in value. If it fails, you might never see that dollar again. Ownership seldom comes with guarantees.

Owners play offense. Loaners play defense. Donors don't get to play.

Most of us will assume all three roles at some point with our money, depending on the circumstances. But how much of your income you decide to put into each category as you earn it will have a huge impact on how successful you are at building wealth. We all have to spend money in our daily lives, but if you choose to spend everything you earn, you won't be able to build wealth. Maintaining your standard will largely depend on your ability to continue working and earning indefinitely to cover your expenses, something most of us would prefer not to consider.

The first step toward True Wealth—digging your financial moat—is a defensive strategy. You need this money to maintain its value, even at the expense of higher returns. For that reason, most of the investments you choose for the Reserve will be conservative in nature and focused more on stability and income generation versus capital appreciation.

These defensive investments typically involve lending your money to some other entity, such as federal and state governments, governmental agencies, municipalities, and corporations. The bonds and similar vehicles issued by these institutions are generally referred to as *fixed-income* investments because they typically pay a fixed rate of interest for a specified period.

When you purchase a bond, it comes with a legal obligation from the issuer to return the face value of your investment to you at maturity in addition to whatever interest you receive while you own it. In many cases, you also have the option of selling the bond to another buyer before the maturity date, but while the face value might be assured, the market price of your investment is not.

What's the risk of focusing too much of your portfolio on defense? To use another sports analogy, you might have the best defensive players in all of baseball on your roster, but if they're not adept at hitting and scoring runs—offensive skills—you won't win many games. Similarly, an investment portfolio that focuses too heavily on defensive, fixed-income investments might not grow enough over time to allow you to reach your financial goals on schedule.

To earn the returns you need, you will likely need to play offense with most of the money you save and invest, and offensive investments almost always involve *owning* something. You might own a little hardware store on the corner or perhaps just a few shares of stock—*fractional* ownership—in a global chain of hardware stores. In both instances, we say you have an *equity* stake in the business, another word for ownership, all or in part. That's why stocks are also referred to as *equities*, a term we will be using extensively from now on.

Whether you own an entire business or a single share of stock, the concept is the same. You assume the risks of ownership in exchange for a claim to all or part of the profits that the business generates. Any business owner will tell you that success is never guaranteed, and thankfully there is also no theoretical limit to how much your ownership stake might eventually appreciate in value. As an equity owner, you now have a financial stake in how well the company is run, how it grows, and ultimately the extent to which it succeeds or fails.

As an investor, you will need to play both offense and defense, by being both an owner and a loaner. Your Reserve portfolio (defense) will be made up of cash and fixed-income vehicles. And your Equity portfolio (offense), will involve owning stocks in some form.

How much you should allocate to each category—Reserve or Equity—will be a simple decision once you grasp this simple but essential concept: ***Every dollar in your portfolio should be invested based on when you plan to spend it in the future.***

You might have a financial emergency tomorrow and need cash immediately. That's an extremely short-term goal that requires low volatility and liquidity. Those funds should be in the Reserve account.

If your daughter starts college next fall, the money you've saved for her next four years of tuition should also be in the Reserve. You could potentially earn more by investing this money in stocks, but with short- or intermediate-term goals you can't afford the risk of a big market downturn just before you need the money.

By contrast, you don't need the day-to-day stability that fixed-income investments offer for money that you plan to spend 20 years from now, such as expenses in retirement. Long-term goals afford you the luxury of playing offense and earning the potentially higher returns that equities have historically offered. That money belongs in the Equity portfolio, at least until your long-term goals become shorter-term goals through the passage of time.

INVESTING THE RESERVE FUND

The purpose of your Reserve portfolio is not to make you rich, but to keep you from being poor. For that reason, earning big returns on this money is not necessary. Here is what you should focus on, in order of priority:

1. Low volatility

2. Liquidity

3. Rate of return

The Reserve is designed to do two things: (1) to help you recover quickly from financial emergencies, and (2) to fund short- and intermediate-term spending goals. If you lose your job or face a major expense that's not part of your monthly spending plan, you'll have ready access to funds to get you through without going into debt. And if that day ever comes, you want all of the money to be there when you need it.

Low volatility is a relative term that means different things to different people. For our purposes, it means defensive investments whose prices are reasonably stable. Short-term fixed-income vehicles, such as bonds from highly rated issuers, generally fit the bill. Remember, you are lending your money to these people, and you don't want to have to worry about getting it back, if and when you ever need it.

> "It's not return *on* my money I'm interested in; it's return *of* my money."
> —MARK TWAIN

Liquidity means having access to your money without delay, something else you shouldn't have to worry about with most of your Reserve funds. Securities issued by the U.S. Treasury, for example, are backed by the full faith and credit of the United States, and they are considered free from default risk, which satisfies our safety requirement.

But what would happen if you bought a bond that matures 30 years from now because it pays an attractive interest rate, and you later needed some or all of the money for an emergency? You would likely be forced to sell the bond before it matures, and if market interest rates have risen since your original purchase, your bond would probably be worth less than you paid for it.

That's because of a natural, inverse relationship between interest rates and bond values. If rates go up, the value of existing bonds goes down, something known as *interest-rate risk*. Longer-term bonds are more sensitive to this risk than shorter-term bonds. Of course, this relationship works both ways: if interest rates *decrease*, bond values rise. Remember, however, that our goal for the Reserve is low volatility first. For that reason, I generally recommend you focus on fixed-income investments with relatively short maturities, generally five years or less.

Rate of return refers to what you earn on an investment while you own it. With fixed-income investments, most if not all of the return will likely come in the form of regular interest payments. This is usually expressed in terms of *yield*. For example, if you buy a bond or similar investment at its face value of $1,000 that promises to pay you $30 per year in interest, we say its stated yield is 3% ($30 annual interest divided by $1,000 face value).

All other things being equal, it's reasonable to assume that the less volatility and greater liquidity you demand from an investment, the lower its yield or rate of return is likely to be. That's a fair and necessary trade-off in our case, because having money available in an emergency is more important to us than the rate of return that we might receive on it.

Keeping stacks of cash in a locked safe might satisfy the first two criteria of the Reserve, but over time the money will begin to lose *purchasing power* to inflation, a risk that investors often overlook. At an inflation rate of just 3% per year, each dollar you save today will have only 54 cents in purchasing power 20 years from now, and just 40 cents after 30 years. To overcome this risk, you'll need to earn a rate of return over time that keeps up with inflation.

So how should you invest your Reserve? First, keep it reasonably safe from default and interest-rate risk. Second, keep it liquid. And third, if at all possible, try to earn a rate of return comparable to inflation over the long run. As you dig your moat and build the Reserve, I believe a low-cost mutual fund or exchange-traded fund* that invests in a diversified portfolio of high-quality fixed-income investments with short-term maturities might serve your needs. As you approach True Wealth, we will develop a more refined strategy for your Reserve, but for now let's keep it simple and easy.

BRING OUT THE OFFENSE

The Reserve is pure defense. To move forward, you need offense.

Let me emphasize again that building wealth almost always involves *owning* something. It could be a chain of dry-cleaning stores. It might

---

* Mutual funds are investment vehicles that pool assets from shareholders to invest in stocks, bonds, and/or other securities. Exchange-traded funds, or ETFs, operate much like mutual funds, but their shares are purchased and sold on securities exchanges similar to the way stocks are traded.

be an internet business you run from a laptop in your spare time. Or it could be a stock or mutual fund portfolio you build through monthly savings deposits. In each example, you assume some risk in exchange for the potential of making a profit. No guarantees, no limits.

Your Equity portfolio represents your offensive strategy. Most successful sports franchises involve high-scoring offenses built on a foundation of solid defense, and it's the same with investing. Once you have your Reserve in place, you will need Equity. And that means owning stocks.

When we talk about stocks, we're not referring simply to pieces of paper or numbers on a screen. We're also not talking about "the market." We want to invest the Equity portion of your savings in *profitable businesses.* The stock's price only tells us what we must currently pay to acquire a tiny piece of the business, a *share,* so named because it entitles us to share in the company's future earnings, dividends, and growth potential. Market indexes, such as the Dow Jones Industrial Average, the Standard & Poor's 500, or the Nasdaq Composite index, represent the collective "price" of a broad selection of stocks at a given point in time.

In building an Equity portfolio, we would like to own shares of profitable, well-run, growing companies that are committed to sharing their success in a tangible way with us as owners. We want to acquire a stake in these wonderful businesses at attractive prices relative to their underlying values. And while we need to be careful and selective, we ultimately want to own a whole bunch of them.

Owning stocks (equities) is like owning any business: It involves risks. Thankfully, there are ways to mitigate those risks, some of which we have already discussed and others that we will explore in the chapters ahead. But first, let's try to understand why it's worth taking those risks in the first place.

THE CASE FOR EQUITIES

Contrary to what you often hear, our world is becoming a better and better place to live. We've got some fairly serious problems, of course, and many people will be happy to tell you all about them when you ask—and sometimes even when you don't. But the evidence is clear that despite those challenges, our long, upward climb is still very much underway.

If you can't see it, it's probably not that you're too far away—but that you're too close.

Remember the man with the yo-yo walking up the hill? You might be focusing on the yo-yo and missing the hill. You might look at the world today and see all of its many problems: crime, hunger, jobless-ness, the environment, inequality, racial injustice—all serious issues indeed. You might see them as signs that civilization is in an irrevers-ible decline—as it is often portrayed in the media—while ignoring the progress that has been made in each of those areas over time. By focus-ing solely on today's challenges—as serious as they are and will always likely be in some form—you are missing humankind's slow march up the hill.

Opportunities and wealth are still being created where they were once stifled and limited. A rising middle class is emerging, and what its members now think of as daily necessities were once considered luxu-ries, even among the ultra-wealthy.

John D. Rockefeller, the richest American who ever lived, didn't have central air-conditioning, television, or penicillin. Or Starbucks.

Through their own initiative, hard work, and thrift, billions of our neighbors around the world pursue their own dreams. The money they earn is helping successive generations climb even higher. And with breathtaking advances in technology and productivity, their efforts are being multiplied. One by one, problems created by human-kind are being solved by humankind.

Has it ever occurred to you that most of this technology and inno-vation seems to come from those parts of the world where economic freedom, competition, and rewards are the greatest? Do you see a connection? Can you imagine it continuing? And if so, how do you plan to participate?

> "In the long run, people behave in keeping with their basic impulse to become: to be, to do, and to own. Technological progress compounds—exponentially, per Moore's Law—in response to the eagerness of the free market to reward it. The spirit of entrepreneurism and innovation continues to arise, and to thrive, in ever larger parts of the world. And publicly-owned companies strive ceaselessly to increase their revenues, earnings, cash flows, and dividends on behalf of their shareholders."
>
> **—NICK MURRAY**

Of all the different ways there are to invest, I believe equities are the only investment class that truly and fully captures human ingenuity and progress. For that reason, equities have generated returns over time greatly in excess of their fixed-income counterparts. Owners tend to do better than loaners, and both do better than donors.

Progress follows no rigid schedule, however; uncertainties persist, and equity returns can't be guaranteed. In the short run especially, stock prices can often be volatile, and owning them will tax your patience. As an investor, your own emotions are the greatest threat you face. And as an owner of equities, your success will likely correspond to your ability to act in opposition to those emotions. Prices will fluctuate as they always have—that's called volatility—and giving in to your emotions by selling your stocks is often what turns temporary declines into permanent losses. If you can avoid making that mistake, there are ways that volatility can even help you compound wealth even faster.

A key point to understand is that volatility—the day-to-day inconsistency of equity prices—*is actually what creates their higher returns over time.* What kind of person would consciously choose to accept more uncertainty from an investment without expecting to be compensated for it?

WHAT RISK IS, AND WHAT IT ISN'T

Many investors make the mistake of assuming that volatility is the same thing as risk. It makes sense to them to minimize risk however they can, either by avoiding equities altogether or by trying to own them at the "right time."

When a stock leaps in price one day and drops sharply the next, that's not risk. It's volatility. It's simply what stocks do, and short-term volatility is the price investors pay for the superior return equities have historically delivered over long time periods. Think of it this way: Volatility is the likelihood of being *surprised and/or disappointed* by an investment on any given day. And if you choose to track the performance of your equity portfolio daily, you're going to be disappointed fairly often. History tells us, however, that the longer you own equities, the less likely you are to be disappointed in their eventual returns.

Imagine an investment whose value declines every year by 2% to 3% on average. You purchase it for $100, and a year later it's worth $98. The following year it's down to $95, and then $93, then $91 and so on, slowly but persistently losing value. Would you call that a *volatile* investment? Not at all: The returns seem largely consistent year-to-year. Would you call an investment that consistently loses 2% to 3% of its value nearly every year *risky*?

Yes, and so would I. And to see how much of it you own right now, just look in your wallet.

The people who consider cash to be a risk-free investment are likely to be the same people who believe stocks are risky. Holding cash allows them to avoid volatility and makes them feel safe, but the longer they hold it, the more its purchasing power inevitably gets eaten away by inflation.

Equity investors, on the other hand, understand that the prices of their investments will fluctuate constantly, unpredictably, and sometimes wildly. But history tells them that the longer they hold stocks—the more day-to-day disappointments they can withstand—the more likely they will be rewarded over time for their patience and discipline.

Not to oversimplify it, but volatility isn't risk. It's opportunity.

So if volatility isn't risk, then what is? When it comes to investing, I can think of two definitions. The first is to think of risk as **the possibility of permanent loss.** If you own stock in a company that fails, you might lose your entire investment. Thankfully that doesn't happen very often, but business risk is real, which is why the companies you invest in should be of very high quality. You should also own several of them, for reasons we will explore in later chapters.

You can also experience permanent loss if you allow your emotions to guide your investment decisions. If the next market downturn causes you to panic and sell shares for less than you paid for them in order to ease your emotional pain, you will be converting temporary volatility into permanent loss. That is risk realized. Understand, however, that the market only created the volatility. *You* created the risk—and the loss.

But what if you are in a situation where you *have* to sell stocks simply because you need the money? This could also result in permanent losses, but it might also be among the easiest risks to manage. As you will learn, any money you *plan* to withdraw from your portfolio over at least the next five years shouldn't be in equities in the first place; that's what short-term fixed-income investments are for. And unforeseen, *unplanned* expenditures should also come from the Reserve. Stocks are no place for your spending money.

The second definition of financial risk—and my favorite—is **the possibility that you won't achieve your goals.** If you want to build wealth over time and eventually achieve True Wealth, then the higher returns historically offered by equities should increase your chances of achieving it, assuming of course that you have the patience and discipline to allow it to happen. But if your investment strategy is based on avoiding volatility at all costs, it won't likely deliver the investment returns you need to reach your goal. That's just risk in another form.

Retirees who insist on avoiding the volatility of equities could at some point find themselves devouring more and more of their investment capital each year if they aren't able to earn enough to replace their rising withdrawals.

They might even run out of money one day, but at least they'll do it "safely."

TAKEAWAYS:

- Make the transition from saver to investor as soon as you are able.

- Compounding is the key to building wealth, and it can start with the first dollar you invest.

- There are no shortcuts to True Wealth.

- Set priorities to invest more productively.

- To build wealth, be an owner, instead of a loaner or donor.

- Keep your Reserve fund in liquid, low-volatility investments.

- Invest in equities to build wealth over time.

- Volatility isn't risk. Risk is the possibility of permanent loss. It's also the possibility that you won't reach your financial goals.

CHAPTER 6

BUILDING WEALTH THROUGH DOLLAR-COST AVERAGING

B eing an owner of equities means accepting, even embracing, volatility as the price we pay for the attractive returns that stocks have historically provided over long time periods. In exchange, we also enjoy the possibility that those advantages might continue in the future.

But what if you could actually *transform* volatility—the day-to-day fluctuation in stock prices—from an annoying distraction into an *advantage*, and in the process possibly even earn a higher rate of return than the very investments you own?

TURNING VOLATILITY TO YOUR ADVANTAGE

When it comes to building wealth, that scenario is indeed possible. And investors who understand and follow the simple strategy I'm about to describe have been taking advantage of the possible benefits for decades. The idea is so deceptively simple, however, that it gets overlooked by those who have bought into the notion that investment success requires complexity, overthinking, and/or shortcuts.

It works in part by removing human emotion from investment decisions. Instead, you are required to do the same things repeatedly, without deliberation, regardless of market conditions.

And the best part? The more volatile the investment, the better the strategy works.

We're talking about *dollar-cost averaging*, a well-known strategy that you might already be familiar with. In fact, if you have been systematically investing a portion of every paycheck through a retirement plan at work, you're probably following the strategy without even realizing it. Dollar-cost averaging, or DCA as many investors refer to it, has been around so long that no one even knows who invented it. It's based on some very simple, easy-to-understand arithmetic, and yet it's one of the most powerful investment strategies ever conceived.

There is nothing magic about dollar-cost averaging. It won't help you choose the best investments. It won't keep you from losing money, and it has some built-in weaknesses that even some who swear by it don't fully understand. But if you are trying to build wealth one deposit at a time, I know of no other approach that works as well, and there are ways to overcome its limitations.

**Dollar-cost averaging simply means investing equal
dollar amounts into the same investment vehicle
at regular intervals. That's all there is to it.**

If you arrange to have $500 a month drafted from your checking account on the same day each month and invested in shares of the same mutual fund, you are dollar-cost averaging.

If you purchase $1,000 worth of your favorite company's shares in the first week of every quarter—regardless of the price—you are dollar-cost averaging.

If you save 10% of every paycheck through your employer's 401(k) plan and have it split among five different plan options, you are dollar-cost averaging—times five.

Now let's explore how dollar-cost averaging works with some hypothetical examples. More importantly, let's try to understand exactly *why* it works.

DCA WHEN PRICES ARE VOLATILE

If there's one thing you can almost always count on with stocks, it's that their prices tend to zig and zag, up and down, sometimes for no clear reason other than that's what stocks do. And sometimes, despite all the bouncing around, those prices can wind up right where they started, weeks, months, possibly even years later.

When prices seem to fluctuate without any clear direction up or down for a time, investors refer to this as a *sideways* market. This happens more often than you might think, and it doesn't sound like a recipe for making money grow. But let's see how dollar-cost averaging might help you.

In the following hypothetical example, you're automatically investing $1,000 on the same day each month in a single stock, mutual fund, or exchange-traded fund (ETF), buying however many shares you can based on the current price at the time:

Month	You Invested	Share Price	Shares Bought	Shares Owned	Portfolio Value
1	$1,000	$50	20.0	20.0	$1,000
2	$1,000	$40	25.0	45.0	$1,800
3	$1,000	$50	20.0	65.0	$3,250
4	$1,000	$60	16.7	81.7	$4,900
5	$1,000	$50	20.0	101.7	$5,083
6	$1,000	$40	25.0	126.7	$5,067
7	$1,000	$50	20.0	146.7	$7,333
8	$1,000	$60	16.7	163.4	$9,800
9	$1,000	$50	20.0	183.4	$9,167

This chart is for illustration purposes only and does not represent an actual investment.

Take a look at Month 1. At the current price of $50 per share, your $1,000 buys you 20 shares. One month later in Month 2, you notice that your fund has dropped in price to $40 per share. But instead of wringing your hands about it, you automatically invest another $1,000, which allows you to buy another 25 shares at the lower price. Every month you faithfully invest the same $1,000 into the same fund, regardless of the price of its shares. No deliberation, no prognostication; you just keep accumulating shares.

After nine months of dollar-cost averaging and back-and-forth share prices, you stop to see how you're doing:

- First, look at the Share Price column above. You began investing when the share price was $50, and nine months later that's exactly where the price ended up. In other words, the *investment* return of your stock or fund has been exactly 0%.

- Over the last nine months, you invested a total of **$9,000** (9 x $1,000). Yet despite the 0% return of your investment vehicle, your *portfolio* has an ending value of **$9,167**. You have somehow managed to outperform your own investment, and your **$167 profit** is entirely the result of dollar-cost averaging.

- Here's *how* that happened. The average *price* of your stock or fund over this time period (the average of all the numbers from the Share Price column above) was **$50**. With your $9,000 investment, you accumulated a total of 183.4 shares (the Shares Owned column). If you divide $9,000 by 183.4 shares, you'll see that your average *cost* for these shares was **$49.10**. In this example, you wound up receiving an average "discount" of **90 cents** on every share you purchased.

- Here's *why* that happened. Notice in the hypothetical illustration above that the *lower* the share price, the *greater* number of shares you were able to buy with your same $1,000 monthly investment. Conversely, the *higher* the share price, the *fewer* shares you were able to purchase. In the end, you own a greater number of "undervalued" shares than "expensive" shares, which brings down your average cost.

Even though the share price ended up exactly where it started, those share prices bounced around quite a bit month to month. That's the classic definition of volatility, which, as we know, many investors fear and try to avoid. But in this hypothetical example, thanks to dollar-cost averaging, the volatility actually worked in your favor and improved your results.

DCA WHEN PRICES ARE RISING

What would happen in the unlikely event that the share price of your investment went *up* every month? Could dollar-cost averaging give you an advantage in this environment as well?

Let's use another hypothetical example: Invest $1,000 on the same day each month in the same stock or fund for the next nine months, regardless of its price. This time, however, the share price *climbs* steadily by five dollars every month:

Month	You Invested	Share Price	Shares Bought	Shares Owned	Portfolio Value
1	$1,000	$30	33.3	33.3	$1,000
2	$1,000	$35	28.6	61.9	$2,167
3	$1,000	$40	25.0	86.9	$3,476
4	$1,000	$45	22.2	109.1	$4,911
5	$1,000	$50	20.0	129.1	$6,456
6	$1,000	$55	18.2	147.3	$8,102
7	$1,000	$60	16.7	164.0	$9,839
8	$1,000	$65	15.4	179.4	$11,658
9	$1,000	$70	14.3	193.7	$13,555

This chart is for illustration purposes only and does not represent an actual investment.

Some observations:

- In this scenario, you again invested a total of **$9,000** over a nine-month period. And the *average* price of your hypothetical investment was **$50** per share, both the same as in the previous example.

- This time, however, you acquired a total of 193.7 shares with an ending value of **$13,555**. That's a **profit** of **$4,555**.

- Your average *cost* was **$46.49** per share, substantially lower than the $50 average *price* over the same period.

- And again, your portfolio wound up being weighted more heavily in lower-price shares and less heavily in higher-price shares. Dollar-cost averaging created that imbalance, and in this hypothetical rising-price environment it again worked to your advantage with no additional effort on your part.

- Would your results have been even better if you had invested the entire $9,000 in the first month? Of course. But when you're trying to build wealth, having a large sum of money available at one time is typically not an option.

DCA WHEN PRICES ARE FALLING

So far it appears that dollar-cost averaging can work well when prices are bouncing around unpredictably, and perhaps even better when prices are consistently rising. But if you're like most people, you worry about the possibility that once you decide to invest, the bottom will fall out. Murphy's Law, perhaps?

So, this time, let's flip those share prices upside-down and see how dollar-cost averaging works when prices *decline* steadily month after month as you're buying shares:

Month	You Invested	Share Price	Shares Bought	Shares Owned	Portfolio Value
1	$1,000	$70	14.3	14.3	$1,000
2	$1,000	$65	15.4	29.7	$1,929
3	$1,000	$60	16.7	46.4	$2,780
4	$1,000	$55	18.2	64.6	$3,549
5	$1,000	$50	20.0	84.6	$4,226
6	$1,000	$45	22.2	106.8	$4,803
7	$1,000	$40	25.0	131.8	$5,270
8	$1,000	$35	28.6	160.4	$5,611
9	$1,000	$30	33.3	193.7	$5,809

This chart is for illustration purposes only and does not represent an actual investment.

How did you do this time?

- Total investment over nine months: **$9,000.** Average price of the investment over that period was the same **$50** per share as in both prior examples.

- You accumulated 193.7 shares, the same number as the rising-price scenario. (This shouldn't be too surprising; the monthly prices were the same but occurred in reverse order.)

- Your average *cost*, then, would also be the same **$46.49.** Again, well below the $50 average *price* per share.

- In fact, there's only one difference between this scenario and the prior one, but it's a big one. Because the price of your hypothetical investment went down every month, your $9,000 total investment became **$5,809**. That's a **$3,191 loss**.

Here we learn something very important about dollar-cost averaging. Even though you were able to buy shares over time at an average cost below the average price of the same investment, DCA did not keep you from losing money. The benefits of dollar-cost averaging are relative, not absolute. The strategy might outperform the investment vehicle you're using it with, but profits are never assured.

Of course, in the falling-price scenario, if and when share prices eventually reversed course and began recovering, you would benefit from the fact that your portfolio was weighted more heavily in shares purchased at lower prices. And in the meantime, just knowing how dollar-cost averaging works might have been enough to keep you from abandoning your strategy altogether when times got tough.

DCA WHEN PRICES DON'T CHANGE

Here's one last hypothetical example of dollar-cost averaging, albeit a pretty unlikely one in the real world. What if you systematically bought shares of an investment over the next nine months—*and the price never changed at all?*

Here's how that would look under the same premises of the other three examples:

Month	You Invested	Share Price	Shares Bought	Shares Owned	Portfolio Value
1	$1,000	$50	20.0	20.0	$1,000
2	$1,000	$50	20.0	40.0	$2,000
3	$1,000	$50	20.0	60.0	$3,000
4	$1,000	$50	20.0	80.0	$4,000
5	$1,000	$50	20.0	100.0	$5,000
6	$1,000	$50	20.0	120.0	$6,000
7	$1,000	$50	20.0	140.0	$7,000
8	$1,000	$50	20.0	160.0	$8,000
9	$1,000	$50	20.0	180.0	$9,000

This chart is for illustration purposes only and does not represent an actual investment.

This one's pretty easy to calculate:

- Total investment: **$9,000** over nine months. Average share *price*: **$50**. Average *cost* per share: **$50**. **Total profit: $0.**

- Of the four hypothetical scenarios we've explored—up, down, sideways, and flat markets—this is the only one where dollar-cost averaging offers no clear advantage.

- Or look at it another way: No volatility, no advantage.

WHAT DCA CAN DO, AND WHAT IT CAN'T

As you have seen, dollar-cost averaging can be an excellent strategy for building wealth, systematically allowing you to buy more shares when they are relatively undervalued and fewer shares when prices are higher.

The concept is easy to understand, and it's simple to set up and follow. It removes emotions, guesswork, and market forecasting from the list of things you have to think about. And while market timing increases the odds of underperforming your own investments, dollar-cost averaging does just the opposite. The more volatile the investment vehicle you choose, the better the strategy can work. Of course, the reverse is also true: The more stable the price of your investment, the less of an advantage DCA provides.

While this strategy might seem ingenious, it's far from perfect. If your investment vehicle declines consistently in price after you buy it, as we saw in one of the hypothetical examples above, all the dollar-cost averaging in the world won't prevent you from losing money.

I would also caution you against using the strategy with large lump sums of money. Spreading your investments out over time might reduce the chances of unfortunate timing, but market history tells us the advantage is likely to be mostly psychological. The longer you delay getting money invested, the less time it has to grow and compound. As powerful as dollar-cost averaging can be, it pays to keep time on your side when you have a lot of money to invest.

Finally, some investors—and even some financial advisors— believe that since DCA is so effective at helping people *accumulate* wealth, that it should work equally well in retirement, when those same investors decide to *withdraw* funds from their portfolios in regular, equal amounts to cover living expenses. But sadly, they are wrong. Dollar-cost averaging still works, but in retirement the strategy works *against* you. Its strengths actually turn into weaknesses.

If you think about it, you will quickly understand why. The key to building wealth through dollar-cost averaging is that, as long as the price of your investment fluctuates, the strategy will allow you to purchase a greater number of shares at relatively low prices and fewer shares at higher prices. In the end, your average cost per share will typically be lower than the average share price of the investment itself over the same time period.

But if you use the same logic when *withdrawing* money, the advantages become disadvantages. The lower the share price when you make your next withdrawal, *the more shares you'll need to liquidate*. The same strategy that helped you build wealth automatically all your life will only make you spend it faster in retirement if you try to follow it in reverse.

That's not dollar-cost averaging. **That's dollar-cost *ravaging*.**

There are much better ways to make money last once you start living off of it than systematically liquidating your life's savings with a flawed approach. We will explore them later.

DCA'S ACHILLES' HEEL

For all of its wealth-building benefits, dollar-cost averaging does suffer from one built-in weakness that even some of its most ardent proponents often overlook. The strategy is inherently vulnerable to something called the Law of Diminishing Returns, which basically means that the longer you do something, the smaller the benefit.

To illustrate, let's look at another example. Say you've been faithfully investing $1,000 each month in an equity mutual fund whose price goes up and down unpredictably. You recognize this as volatility, and you understand that by dollar-cost averaging you can actually turn that volatility to your advantage. Over time, your average cost for the shares you've purchased does indeed turn out to be lower than the average price of the fund over the same time period. DCA is working.

But as your nest egg grows larger with each month's $1,000 deposit, you begin to notice that the gap between the average cost and the average price of the shares you're buying has begun to narrow. The reason is simple: as your total investment grows in size, your $1,000 deposits represent smaller and smaller percentages of the total portfolio.

When you added $1,000 in the second month, it represented 50% of the total invested. But the $1,000 you invested in Month 10 represented just 10% of the total. Your portfolio might be growing in size, but your deposits are staying the same. So every month, your $1,000 has less and less impact on the total portfolio, which means dollar-cost averaging has a smaller and smaller effect on your results.

Ironically, the longer you follow this wonderful strategy, the less it seems to work.

That's not to say you should abandon your plan, however. Dollar-cost averaging can continue to work, but its benefits will slowly diminish as your portfolio grows in size. The only way to maintain its full impact would be to increase the amount of your deposits at the same rate at which your portfolio grows, which is simply not feasible for most investors, at least not for very long.

So, is there any way to continue enjoying the benefits of dollar-cost averaging *without* coming up with more and more money to invest every month? Yes, thankfully there is.

DIVIDENDS ARE THE ANSWER

Successful businesses make money; they generate profits. Companies that don't consistently turn a profit don't seem to stick around for very long. Truly successful companies find ways to grow and become even more successful by putting the profits they earn to work: creating new products and services, finding new customers, and increasing productivity.

As a shareholder, a part owner of a business, some of those profits essentially belong to you. Having a claim on them won't pay for your groceries, however; you'll need cash for that. And if you own stock in a company that shares some of its profits in the form of dividends, you will receive cash—typically quarterly—for every share you own.

While many companies pay regular dividends to their shareholders, they are not obligated to do so. Dividend policy is set at the discretion of the company's board of directors and can be changed at any time.

If you own shares of a company that does decide to pay cash dividends, you get to decide what to do with that money once it's paid to you, and if your goal is to build wealth through dollar-cost averaging, dividends will help maintain the benefits of the strategy.

Here's how:

- With every regular savings deposit, you purchase shares. Dollar-cost averaging gives you the potential to acquire those shares over time at a discount to their average market price.

- When the shares that you own pay dividends, you are able to *add* that cash to the money you're already investing, which allows you to buy even *more* shares.

- The more shares you accumulate, the more dividends you can earn, and the more shares you can buy with that money the next time you invest. At some point, your dividend income might even exceed what you're investing on your own each month.

Adding dividend income to your regular deposits helps maintain the effectiveness of dollar-cost averaging, because it allows your systematic investments to increase over time, and it's a classic example of compounding. It makes your money work for *you* while you're working for *it*. And one day you might discover that you are collecting enough in dividend income to allow you to stop working for money altogether. That's True Wealth.

TAKEAWAYS:

- Although volatility is a given for equity investments, you can make it work for you through dollar-cost averaging.

- As your portfolio grows through dollar-cost averaging, the advantages of the strategy narrow over time.

- Dollar-cost averaging doesn't work in reverse. Systematically withdrawing the same amount of money from an investment requires you to sell more shares when prices are down, turning the strategy's advantage into a liability.

- Reinvesting dividends along with your regular deposits can help overcome the strategy's shortcomings.

CHAPTER 7

USING DIVIDENDS TO BUILD WEALTH

Companies that have long, proven records of consistently paying dividends through good times and bad are telling you something about themselves, and as an investor it will pay you to listen, especially if those dividends tend to increase on a regular basis.

WHY DIVIDEND GROWTH IS KEY

Dividends are paid out of profits, and we like profitable businesses. That's not to say that a company can't pay dividends in a year that it posts a loss, but it can't keep up the practice indefinitely without some serious negative consequences. In a general sense, a long track record of consistent dividend payments often implies an equally long record of profitability. That's a good thing.

Profits, on the other hand, can be subject to interpretation and occasionally to manipulation. It's been said that profits are a matter of opinion; dividends are a matter of fact. You might need an accounting degree to figure out exactly how a company calculates its earnings in a given quarter, but there's no guesswork when it comes to dividends. They are paid in cash, and when that cash flows into your investment account, it's real money, and it's yours.

A consistent policy of paying dividends—and *increasing* them over time—also imposes a measure of fiscal discipline on management. Knowing that some portion of the company's annual earnings have been pledged to shareholders, managers are forced to make better decisions. They may think twice about squandering profits on risky acquisitions or other questionable allocations of capital.

Finally, dividends can signal to investors the degree of confidence management has in the business itself. If managers and directors are pessimistic about the future, they might be reluctant to pay dividends—much less to increase them—preferring instead to hoard cash in anticipation of tough times ahead or, worse, a long-term decline. Increasing dividends can be an indicator of sound financial health and a signal that management expects it to continue.

As part owner of a business that is committed and able to pay increasing dividends over time, you stand to benefit in several ways:

- Dividends allow you to benefit from compounding. In fact, rising dividends are a form of compounding *within* compounding, allowing you the potential to build wealth faster than you otherwise might.

- Dividends extend and enhance the benefits of dollar-cost averaging.

- When you reach the point in life when you choose to stop working for money, dividends can represent a stream of rising income to help cover your spending needs. And if the cash flow from dividends rises faster than your cost of living, you'll be able to maintain or even increase your standard of living.

- Finally, dividends make it easier for you to ignore the unpredictable day-to-day fluctuations in the value of your investments. The truth is—as you will see in the next few pages—dividends not only lessen the negative impact of market downturns, but they can also help you recover from them sooner.

BUILDING WEALTH WITH DIVIDENDS

When stock prices do inevitably turn down, your portfolio will not be immune. Contrary to popular opinion, however, this is far from the end of the world. In fact, if your goal is to build wealth, falling stock prices could be one of the best things that ever happen to you.

Why? For one thing, history tells us that while market pullbacks have occurred fairly frequently over the last hundred years or so, they have also been temporary.

Second, stock prices and dividends are not directly connected. If you own shares in a quality business with a record of consistent dividend increases, there's no reason to believe that the dividend will be reduced or eliminated just because the stock price has dropped.

And third, market downturns give you the opportunity to buy more shares at lower prices. Remember how dollar-cost averaging works?

If you are going to own equities—and I trust by now that you will—you must assume that prices overall will decline by 10% or more every year or two. And if history is any guide, every six or seven years on average, you should expect something even more severe.

When stock prices drop by more than 20% overall, it's called a *bear market*. And when the media are shouting from the rooftops that financial Armageddon is upon us, it can be pretty scary. For the uninitiated, a bear market is a reason to panic. For the rest of us, *it's a sale.*

If you can keep your head when those about you are losing theirs, bear markets can actually *help* you accumulate wealth. In a market sell-off, stock prices fall almost across the board, including those in your portfolio, but the dividend income you continue to receive will help to cushion the blow. You will use that income, along with your regular savings deposits, to buy even more shares of the companies you own at better prices. And if your companies keep increasing their dividends, the income benefit of bargain prices is magnified. More shares multiplied by rising dividends equals greater income.

Then at some point, unknowable in advance to you or anyone else, the market stops falling. The bear market ends, the crisis abates, and the next bull market quietly begins. The prices of your shares begin to recover, and your investment return is enhanced by the extra shares you have accumulated through dividend reinvestment. And guess what? All of those newly acquired shares are now earning dividends of their own.

> "I can't emphasize enough the importance of dividends and reinvesting those dividends. You'll find that dividend payers that trade at reasonable valuations are stocks that did the very best for investors over the long run."
> **—JEREMY SIEGEL**

Remember, compounding takes time. A farmer plants a seed, waters, and fertilizes it. But for weeks, sometimes months, there is nothing to show for his efforts. All of the early growth takes place underground, out of sight. It takes time, patience, and a good deal of faith born of experience for the farmer to see results.

Likewise, the benefits of compounding dividend income are almost impossible to see in the short run but impossible to ignore in the long run.

Knowing all of this gives you a tremendous psychological edge as an investor:

- The rising stream of income your investments produce makes it easier to handle price fluctuations, especially when you understand how volatility can help you build wealth.

- If you are able to focus on the income your portfolio generates, you will at some point start seeing noticeable signs of progress, even when share prices are falling.

- Rising dividends give you a tangible way to measure your progress toward True Wealth as your portfolio income edges closer to what it will take to support your chosen lifestyle once you stop working.

But your money won't stop working just because you do. The same dividends that helped you create wealth will one day also help you pay your bills. And as long as those dividends increase faster than your cost of living over time, it's entirely possible that you will never find yourself having to sell shares to finance your lifestyle.

If that's the case, it won't matter quite so much what stock prices—or even the value of the shares you own—are doing at any given moment. You won't have to play the hopeless game of guessing what will happen next to the economy or the financial markets. And you'll never again have to pay attention to people who make a living trying to scare you into making bad decisions.

THE DIVIDEND METHOD

Building a portfolio of stocks that pay dividends and consistently increase them gives you three important ways to build wealth: (1) you get dividend income **now** that you can reinvest in additional shares; (2) to the extent that your companies increase their dividends, you get additional income **later**, which helps preserve the benefits of dollar-cost averaging;

and (3) while never guaranteed, there is always the potential that your shares—and your portfolio—can appreciate in value over time.

Capital appreciation is a wonderful thing, but it's actually not essential to making your plan work. The Dividend Method involves building a diversified portfolio of companies over time by saving 15% of your annual income and letting dividends help you accumulate even more shares through dollar-cost averaging and compounding. Once you achieve True Wealth, under whatever terms you choose to define it, you will open the tap and start spending some or all of those dividends as you receive them. In the meantime, just remember that it's the total cash flow from your investments that will allow you to stop working for money one day, not the size of your portfolio.

If you are building your Equity portfolio from scratch, I believe you may want to invest through a diversified equity mutual fund or exchange-traded fund (ETF) that will allow you to make small, regular deposits. If you can make these fund purchases *automatically* each month, so much the better. Because these funds typically hold a large number of stocks across several industries, you gain instant diversification. Regular deposits into a single fund will also allow you to see the benefits of dollar-cost averaging more clearly. Using a fund may also be a less expensive option compared with the transaction costs often associated with buying shares of individual stocks, at least initially.

Once your portfolio reaches critical mass, however, I encourage you to begin building your own portfolio of individual companies based on the Dividend Method selection criteria explained in the next several sections. There are a couple of ways to approach this—either incrementally or all at once when your fund reaches a certain size—but you will want to transition eventually into shares of about **25 companies** in roughly equal dollar amounts.

It's important to keep your portfolio diversified, which helps to spread the risk of having too much concentrated in a single industry or sector. The research firm Standard & Poor's divides the U.S. economy into 11 different equity sectors. Here's a list of them, along with examples of the types of companies they include:

- Communication Services (media, entertainment, interactive media companies)

- Consumer Discretionary (cars, jewelry, electronics retailers, restaurant chains)

- Consumer Staples (food and beverage companies, household and personal product providers)

- Energy (oil and gas exploration, refining, fuel transportation)

- Financials (banks, credit card issuers, insurance, investment companies)

- Health care (medical supplies and devices, pharmaceutical companies)

- Industrials (airlines, railroads, aerospace, defense contractors)

- Information Technology (internet, computers, other technology-based companies)

- Materials (providers of raw materials, such as lumber, metals, plastic, paper, concrete)

- Real Estate (real estate investment trusts, other realty companies)

- Utilities (water, electricity, and gas providers)

It's not necessary to own stocks from every sector but do try to limit your holdings in any one of the above sectors to no more than **30% of your total Equity portfolio.** This means no more than seven of your 25 companies would be in the same sector. A diversified stock portfolio should be like a well-planned flower garden; it's more likely you will always see something in bloom.

As you begin selecting stocks for your portfolio, understand that you will be going into partnership with these companies in a very real sense. And as with the choice of any partner—business or otherwise—there are certain standards you'll want them to meet.

The Dividend Method involves selecting individual equities based on six important standards: quality, financial strength, growth, dividend sustainability, current yield, and value. We will explore these standards one by one to see why they are so important.

Before we begin, understand that researching and selecting individual securities for your portfolio can be time consuming and laborious. For many it will be a labor of love, and, if that's you, I hope the following pages will guide you in making wise investment decisions. If you prefer to delegate this task to someone else, use these general guidelines in conversations with your financial advisor, or look for mutual funds or ETFs that follow a similar strategy.

STANDARD #1: Quality

Your search for portfolio candidates should always begin with quality. We want to go into partnership with businesses that we believe will be around for a lifetime, and it's entirely possible that you will own shares in these companies for decades to come.

Start the process by understanding how the company makes money. Does it make a product or provide a service that will likely be in demand for the long term—or is it just another fad company making a fad product in a fad industry that won't survive the next shift in consumer preferences? It's tempting to fall in love with a story—a new technology, a medical breakthrough, the latest fashion trend—but if the company doesn't have a second act, if it can't continue to innovate, expand its customer base, and/or increase its prices, then it likely won't make for a good long-term investment.

> "It's far better to buy a wonderful company at a
> fair price than a fair company at a wonderful price."
> **—WARREN BUFFETT**

Personally, I like companies that have recurring-revenue business models. That means they sell their products and services to repeat customers, over and over again. Instead of making giant air filtration machines that last for 20 years, for example, they make filters for those machines that have to be replaced every six months. Instead of selling large-scale computer hardware systems, they sell renewable contracts to service those systems.

Recurring-revenue businesses typically have lower capital needs and focus on products and services that are replaced, renewed, restocked, or refilled on a regular basis. And the more a company is successful at creating recurring revenues, the more consistent its annual earnings tend to be, and the easier it is to assess the value of the business.

It's not enough that the company knows how to make money, however. To paraphrase Ben Franklin, how successful is the business at making money *on the money it makes?* We would like management to share some of those annual profits with us in the form of regular and rising cash dividends, but what happens with the rest of those earnings each year? Are they reinvested wisely in ways that will make the business grow, or are they squandered on suspect acquisitions, stock options for executives, or wasteful spending?

A couple of useful profitability indicators are the company's *return on equity (ROE)* and *return on invested capital (ROIC)*. You will find these numbers reported on a variety of financial web sites, such as Yahoo! Finance, Google Finance, and Morningstar, as well as in more traditional research publications such as *Value Line* and *Standard & Poor's* (S&P), which are available in the reference sections of many public libraries or by subscription. ROE and ROIC are calculated somewhat differently, and one or the other may be more applicable to a specific company you are researching, depending on its financial structure and industry. Ideally, we're looking for returns that generally are rising, consistent year over year, and above the industry average.

Some professional research firms also provide ratings on a company's overall quality. Standard & Poor's, for example, assigns an "Earnings and Dividend Quality Rank" to several hundred of the companies it follows. Rankings of A+, A, and A- are considered above average in quality. B+ is considered average, while rankings of B, B-, and C are considered below average. As a starting point in your research, **I suggest focusing on companies with an S&P quality ranking of B+ (average) or higher.**

STANDARD #2: Financial Strength

Financially strong companies have an advantage over their competitors. They are able to generate sufficient cash flow to meet their short-term and long-term obligations without excessive borrowing. This, in turn, gives them the flexibility they need in order to adapt to—and often take advantage of—changing business conditions.

Successful businesses can build strong balance sheets to help protect them in difficult times, not unlike the idea of digging a financial "moat" like yours. The company's size, unique competitive advantages, exposure to business risk, cash reserves, liquidity, debt levels, credit rating, and earnings track record are all useful measurements of its financial strength.

A knowledge of accounting and the ability to interpret balance sheets and income statements will help you assess the financial strength of companies you are thinking of investing in. There are, however, some useful resources that can be used as reasonable substitutes for in-depth security analysis, and I often use them myself. *Value Line,* for example, assigns financial strength ratings to the approximately 1,700 companies that make up *The Value Line Investment Survey*. There are nine steps: A++, A+, A, B++, B+, B, C++, C+, and C. **I recommend sticking with companies rated B+ (average) or higher as you search for portfolio candidates.**

STANDARD #3: Growth

A business can only consistently increase its dividends over many years if its earnings are rising as well. It stands to reason, then, that we want to own shares of companies that steadily increase both their dividends *and* earnings, while having the potential to continue doing so in the future. The research resources mentioned above routinely calculate and publish growth rates for the companies they follow, typically every quarter. Security analysts from Wall Street firms will project future growth rates as well.

As you search for candidates for your portfolio, start with companies that have been consistently profitable—*no annual losses*—for at least the past ten years. Ideally, we would also like to see earnings growing faster than inflation for the last one, five, and 10-year periods. We then apply the same standards to dividend growth. It's also a plus to see *future* earnings and dividends projected to grow faster than inflation, but bear in mind that projections are simply educated guesses based on what analysts perceive about the company.

Occasionally, during recessions and other lean periods, a company may decide not to increase its dividend for a year or two in order to preserve cash. This is acceptable, as long as historical growth rates continue to meet your standards. If the dividend stays flat for more than three years, however, proceed with caution. And if the company has actually *reduced or eliminated* its annual dividend at any point over the last 15 years, move on to another candidate without delay.

STANDARD #4: Dividend Sustainability

Dividends are never guaranteed. They are paid at the discretion of a company's board of directors, and the board can change its mind at any time. Big changes to dividend policy send a signal to investors, however, and they are rarely made on a whim.

A company can reduce or eliminate its dividend for many reasons, from short-term cash flow challenges to major shifts in long-term priorities. Earnings growth might be slowing as the business matures, the company might be altering strategy to remain competitive, or perhaps the firm is facing some form of financial hardship. Whatever the reason, as investors we would prefer the dividend keep heading north instead of south, or worse yet, disappearing altogether.

Several indicators can help you determine whether future dividend increases are likely or if their sustainability is in doubt. In the end, it all boils down to the company's ability to generate profits consistently over time and how it decides to spend them.

The first indicator is how stable earnings have been year over year. If the company is in a cyclical industry—steel, construction, airlines, for example—its profits generally rise and fall with the overall business cycle. This not only lessens the likelihood of consistent dividend increases, but can also make the company more difficult to analyze and understand. Businesses with stable earnings that are growing at sustainable rates tend to be more capable of paying predictable dividends and increasing them in future years. You will more likely find companies such as these in industries that are *noncyclical*, meaning that their earnings are not greatly impacted by the business cycle. Airlines are cyclical; toothpaste is noncyclical.

The second thing to look at is what's known as the *payout ratio*. If a company pays out half of this year's earnings to shareholders in the form of a dividend, we say its payout ratio is 50%. Acceptable payout ratios vary among industries, but clearly anything approaching 100% would be cause for concern. There might, of course, be years when business is unusually slow—or expenses are unusually high—that cause earnings to fall and the payout ratio to spike temporarily. This can happen to any business from time to time, and as long as earnings recover quickly there may be little cause for concern. It is worth further research, however, to determine if the drop in earnings is a onetime occurrence or possibly representative of a longer-term challenge that could threaten future dividend increases.

Many analysts and investors also calculate the payout ratio using a company's *cash flow*. They argue that earnings are much more subject to interpretation and manipulation, while cash flow might give a clearer picture of how much of the company's profits are actually coming in the form of spendable cash. That makes sense, given that dividends are typically also paid in cash. You'll find annual cash flow figures in some of the same resources you use to research earnings and dividends.

What should be more concerning to you are negative *trends* in both the payout ratio and the rate of growth in both earnings and dividends. As businesses mature, it's natural to see growth rates begin to slow and payout ratios gradually rise. But when either of these trends reach extremes, you should pay attention and reconsider the investment.

Here are some warning signs:

- A payout ratio that is significantly higher than the industry average

- A sharply rising trend in the payout ratio over the last 10 years

- One-year growth rates in earnings and/or dividends that are significantly lower than the company's five-year growth rates, which are in turn lower than its 10-year rates

- Dividend growth rates that have been consistently and significantly higher than the growth in earnings or cash flow for an extended period

- A deteriorating balance sheet, which will likely be reflected at some point in the company's financial strength and quality ratings

- Prolonged declining trends in the company's annual return on equity (ROE) or return on invested capital (ROIC), both of which are key measures of profitability

Any of these red flags can be an indication that a company's ability to increase its dividends is under pressure. And it goes without saying that it's better to spot them during your research than after you have invested in the stock.

STANDARD #5: Current Yield

A stock's *current dividend yield* tells us in an instant how much we should expect in income from dividends in a year's time. Yield is a simple calculation, yet it contains some vital information when used in the proper context. Too many investors make the simple mistake of assuming the higher the yield, the more attractive the stock, and they are often disappointed.

Dividend yield is calculated by dividing a stock's annual dividend by its current price, expressed as a percentage. If a company pays a $2 dividend per share and the current share price is $50, we say that the current dividend yield is 4% (2 divided by 50). The dividend is normally defined as either the total of what the company has paid in dividends over the past four quarters (trailing dividend), or the most current quarter's dividend multiplied by four (annualized dividend).

You can easily spot the relationship among prices, dividends, and yields using some basic arithmetic. In short, as the share price *increases*, the dividend yield *decreases*, assuming there is no change in the dividend. Conversely, as a stock's price *falls*, its dividend yield *rises*.

Of course, if the dividend does change, the yield moves in the same direction: Raising the dividend increases the current yield, and reducing the dividend lowers the yield, assuming no change in the stock's price. Take a moment to make sure you fully understand these relationships.

They are not difficult to grasp, but they are essential to understanding dividend investing.

If given a choice between two stocks, knowing nothing more than their current dividend yields, would you generally rather receive a higher yield or a lower yield? At face value, we would naturally want the one with the higher current yield, because we expect to get paid more in dividends each year for every dollar we invest. But there is more to it than that, as there is with almost every other investment decision we face.

If you are a long-term investor trying to build wealth and then live off your dividends someday (which is what we've been aiming for), *dividend growth* might be a lot more important to you than today's yield. With a time horizon as short as 15 years, you would earn much more income from a stock yielding 2% today with a dividend growing at 10% per year than you would from owning a stock with *twice* the starting yield but with no dividend growth, all other factors being equal. The advantages are even greater if you are able to reinvest those dividends as you earn them.

Unusually high dividend yields can also be a sign of underlying problems. Has the share price been driven down sharply (increasing the current yield) because the business is failing? Is the company still paying an unsustainable dividend simply to make its shares appear more attractive? Are there enough earnings and cash flow to support the dividend?

As the old saying goes, if it looks too good to be true, it probably is.

Of course, dividend yields can also be too low. Even with dividends that are increasing rapidly every year, it might take decades to collect enough in dividends to make an investment worthwhile if the current yield is minuscule when you make your initial purchase.

Here are some general guidelines on current yield:

- Assuming they meet the rest of our standards, try to buy stocks with dividend yields higher than that of the S&P 500. There are several ways to find the index's current yield—*The Wall*

Street Journal, for example, or web sites such as ycharts.com and multpl.com.

- Don't overreach for yield. Be skeptical of stocks with dividend yields that are greatly above the average of other companies you are researching, especially if the current yield is also much higher than what has been typical for that particular stock.

- Look for stocks that have *both* reasonably attractive current yields and healthy, sustainable dividend growth rates. It's possible to find them, but even that doesn't guarantee success or make them too good to be true. It simply makes them worthy of further research.

STANDARD #6: Value

"Price is what you pay. Value is what you get."

—WARREN BUFFETT

If a company grows over time, it becomes worth more as a business; its *intrinsic value* increases. There are many ways of estimating that value at any given moment, and none is universally accepted. Valuing a business is a vague concept at best, but it's reasonable for us to assume that if its revenues, earnings, and dividends increase over time, so does its value. If you could plot intrinsic value over time on a graph, the line would probably look fairly smooth.

That's not at all the case with the company's stock price, however, which is far more sensitive to daily news events, rumors, or the fickleness of investors who act irrationally at times, as we already know. And that can actually be a good thing for the rest of us.

"Prices fluctuate more than values—so therein lies opportunity."
—JOEL GREENBLATT

Over time, the price of a stock bounces above its intrinsic value to below it and then back again. We have no control over the size of those bounces in either direction nor how quickly the market might correct a misalignment between the price of the stock and its underlying value. Investing is a waiting game that requires patience. And even then, we will often be wrong.

But if you do a decent job of assessing the value of a given company—and buy its shares only when prices are significantly below it—you increase your chances of success while reducing the risk of overpaying. Your goal should be to invest with a reasonable margin of error between the price you pay for a stock and what its actual value is likely to be. Simply put, you want the odds of success to be firmly in your favor, while conceding that all the analysis in the world will never guarantee a profit.

As we begin our search for value, let's revisit the inverse relationship that exists between a stock's price and its dividend yield. If the dividend remains the same and the stock price rises, then its dividend yield falls. And if the price falls, the yield rises. Relatively speaking, we like *higher yields*—within reason—because we get more dividend income per dollar invested than when yields are lower. We would also prefer to buy stocks at relatively *low prices* rather than at high prices. Everyone likes a bargain.

Put another way, we would like to purchase stocks when their dividend yields are *higher* than normal, which might imply that their prices are *lower* than they should be.

But what does that mean, exactly? How high is high, and how low is low? There is a simple approach to answering this question. And while it's no substitute for in-depth security analysis, it will help keep the odds in your favor. It might not give you the exact house address, but it will tell you if you're in the right neighborhood.

If the company you are considering meets the first five standards of the Dividend Method we've discussed, you're already in the right part of town. Your next objective is to minimize the chances that you are overpaying, and one way to do that is to buy the stock near (or even above) the higher end of its "normal" dividend-yield range.

To determine this range, begin by looking up the stock's high and low prices for each of the past 10 years, along with the dividend the company paid in each of those years. Dividing the dividend by the stock's *high* price for a given year will establish the *low* end of the yield range for that year; dividing the dividend by the *low* price will give you the *high*-end yield for the year. Repeat this calculation for each of the past 10 years until you have 10 high-yield numbers and 10 low-yield numbers.

Next, calculate the *average* of the high-yield numbers and then of the low-yield numbers. These two numbers will represent the "normal" dividend yield range for this particular company for the past decade.

Here's a hypothetical example:

Year	High Price ($)		Dividend ($)		Low Yield	Low Price ($)		Dividend ($)		High Yield
1	50	÷	1.00	=	2.0%	32	÷	1.00	=	3.1%
2	40	÷	1.06	=	2.7%	24	÷	1.06	=	4.4%
3	67	÷	1.12	=	1.7%	39	÷	1.12	=	2.9%
4	84	÷	1.19	=	1.4%	48	÷	1.19	=	2.5%
5	69	÷	1.26	=	1.8%	37	÷	1.26	=	3.4%
6	47	÷	1.34	=	2.8%	28	÷	1.34	=	4.8%
7	60	÷	1.42	=	2.4%	33	÷	1.42	=	4.3%
8	82	÷	1.50	=	1.8%	40	÷	1.50	=	3.8%
9	111	÷	1.59	=	1.4%	57	÷	1.59	=	2.8%
10	105	÷	1.69	=	1.6%	47	÷	1.69	=	3.6%
	10-YEAR AVERAGE LOW YIELD:				2.0%	10-YEAR AVERAGE HIGH YIELD:				3.6%

This chart is for illustration purposes only and does not represent an actual investment.

Finally, compare the current dividend yield of the stock you are considering with its average yield range over the past 10 years. In the above example, if the current yield is near or above the high end of the normal yield range (3.6%), it might be a sign that the current price is on the lower end of normal, which would represent value. And a current dividend yield that is near or above the low end of the normal range (2.0%) might signal that the stock is overvalued.

Your ultimate goal is to find: (1) high-quality, growing companies that (2) pay reasonable, consistent, and rising dividends, with (3) above-average yields, (4) priced attractively based on their historical dividend yield range.

THE DIVIDEND TRIPLE PLAY

In investing, the only thing you can truly count on is being surprised—and often. Once you assemble your portfolio, some of the ideas you invested in with the utmost conviction and confidence will turn out to be lackluster performers. And some of the stocks you bought despite your doubts and trepidations will become the stars of your portfolio. Remember what we said early in this book: *It doesn't always make sense. And it doesn't have to make sense to be true.*

The sooner you understand and accept that fact, the easier all of this will be for you.

Things rarely work out exactly the way we expect them to, but you deserve to know what success looks like for an investor in rising-dividend equities. The following example is purely hypothetical and does not represent an actual investment, but it describes in general terms the kind of experience we're after with the stocks we purchase.

Step One: After careful research, you discover a company, XYZ Corp., that satisfies the first five standards of the Dividend Method: quality, financial strength, growth, dividend sustainability, and current yield. Based on the dividend it has paid over the last 10 years, and its high and low prices in each of those years, you calculate that its dividend yield has generally ranged from 2.5% to 4.0%.

At its current price and dividend, the stock is paying a 3.9% yield, near the high end of its normal yield range. You believe at this price that XYZ stock offers: (1) attractive cash flow, (2) upside appreciation potential, and (3) a suitable margin of error. You invest $10,000 in XYZ shares and begin earning $390 in annual dividends with the potential for higher income in the future.

Step Two: You patiently hold this company in your portfolio of 25 stocks, periodically updating your research on it and the rest of your equity holdings, all the while searching for new candidates to consider owning in the future.

Over time the price of XYZ gradually increases, and despite the fact that the company continues to increase its annual dividend, the stock price rises somewhat faster, causing the current dividend yield to decline. Of course, this doesn't have any negative impact on the income you are receiving in XYZ dividends, but as the stock's current yield drifts lower you wonder if its price is catching up with and possibly even surpassing its underlying value. Eventually the yield drops further to 2.3%, which is actually slightly below the lower end of the normal dividend yield range of 2.5%.

Step Three: Your research uncovers a new company, ABC Inc., that meets all of the Dividend Method standards. Its normal dividend yield range is 2.0% to 3.7%, and at the current price, the dividend yield stands at 3.6%. You decide to sell XYZ—at a profit—and buy ABC with the proceeds, in hopes of repeating your success.

With this transaction, you accomplish three things: (1) you replace an investment that's currently yielding 2.3% with one yielding 3.6%, significantly increasing your dividend income; (2) you now own a stock that appears to be a better value, which, if you are proven correct, offers you greater potential for total return; and (3) you lower the overall risk of your portfolio in the process.

Voila! The Dividend Triple Play.

By this point, I shouldn't need to remind you of the following, but I will:

- As nice as all of this sounds, it rarely works as neatly and smoothly as in this hypothetical example. Stock prices can be volatile and unpredictable, much more so than the underlying fundamentals of the companies they represent.

- The process of watching a stock move from the high end of its dividend yield to the low end—when it *does* happen—often takes not weeks or months, but years. That's especially true if the dividend itself keeps increasing, which is exactly what you want to see happen. But at least you are getting paid while you wait.

- Stocks don't care that you own them. A stock's price won't go up simply because you bought it at a good price. In fact, it may go *down* shortly after your purchase simply to annoy you and make you second-guess yourself. It's a test to see if you are a worthy owner, so prove it with your patience.

- Market trends can complicate things. In prolonged bear markets, you may find attractive opportunities all over the place, but it will take courage on your part to buy stocks when everyone else seems to be selling them. And it will take time for even your best decisions to be validated. Conversely, raging bull markets make it much more difficult to find good bargains to add to your portfolio. Be patient and keep beating the bushes, but don't lower your standards.

MANAGING YOUR PORTFOLIO WITH THE DIVIDEND METHOD

Depending on market conditions, it could take quite some time to finish building your Equity portfolio. As I've said before, picking stocks can be a tedious process. But whether you do it on your own or with professional help, it should be rewarding to become intimately familiar with the companies you're going into business with. The ultimate goal is to own 25 stocks in roughly equal dollar amounts, with no more than 30% of the portfolio (seven stocks) concentrated in a single industry.

Again, you might start with a mutual fund or ETF that focuses on rising-dividend companies to give you diversification from the outset, but as you are able, I suggest you begin transitioning from the fund into individual stocks as you see opportunities.

Once the Equity portfolio is fully assembled, you'll need a strategy for managing it going forward. Here are the key issues to consider:

New money. As you build wealth—through earning, saving, and investing—you will need to decide where to put each new savings deposit. First, check your Reserve portfolio to make sure it contains roughly the equivalent of 30% of your income. If not, top it up with your savings deposits. Once it's fully replenished, add your new deposits to the one or two stocks in your Equity portfolio that represent the best value, *that is,* the ones trading nearest the high end of their normal dividend yield range. (See the section on rebalancing below for some specific purchase guidelines.)

As you do this, however, be careful not to become overly concentrated in any single stock position. This will help keep your portfolio properly diversified.

Dividends. As long as you're still working and building wealth, the dividends you receive from your stocks will be an essential element of dollar-cost averaging and compounding. Add this income to your savings deposits and follow the new money process above. Notice that this is different from simply reinvesting dividends back into the companies that paid them. You should reinvest your dividends *where you see the greatest value* among your present holdings, regardless of where those dividends originated. This approach can also assist you in keeping your portfolio in balance.

Once you reach True Wealth, the plan is to stop reinvesting dividends and start living on them if you choose. We'll discuss this later in the book. Until you get there, let the money that money *makes* continue to make money for you.

Ongoing research. At least once each month, update your research on every stock that you own. Note the current yield and how it compares with the normal yield range you have calculated for that company. Review the other Dividend Method standards that originally led you to purchase shares: quality, financial strength, growth, dividend sustainability, and current yield. Look for significant changes and note anything you want to keep an eye on.

You should also be spending some time looking at new candidates for the Equity portfolio. To use another sports analogy, it's important to keep a close eye on your current roster of 25 stocks, but you should also be developing your "farm team" at the same time. These might be companies that currently meet most but not all of the Dividend Method criteria.

Replacing stocks. So, what happens when you find a compelling new idea for your Equity portfolio? How do you promote a company from the farm team to the Top 25? Once you've decided to add this new stock to your portfolio, identify candidates for replacement within your current holdings—and that *doesn't* simply mean those whose recent performance might be disappointing you.

Here are some reasons that might justify replacing a stock you own:

- Reduction or elimination of the dividend

- Deterioration in any of the Dividend Method standards you used when you initially invested

- Current dividend yield near the low end of the stock's normal range (a sign it could be overvalued), especially if it's lower than the yield of the stock you want to purchase

- A large merger or acquisition that makes it difficult to assess the merits of the company going forward

Once you've identified your least attractive position, replace it with the new one, as long as it doesn't push your holdings in any single sector above 30%.

While prolonged downturns and bear markets might make other investors nervous and afraid, you should view them as opportunities to upgrade the quality of your overall portfolio. In challenging times, it should be easier to find companies you want to own, and you might be able to lock in some attractive dividend yields in the process. Another added benefit: If you are staying current with your research, you'll probably be too busy looking for new ideas to worry about what's going on in the market.

Rebalancing. Some investors follow a very strict, statistical approach to managing equities, insisting that each holding be kept precisely at a given percentage, or "weighting" within the portfolio. This is called *rebalancing*, and it can be a profitable portfolio management strategy. There is some wisdom in mechanically trimming a position that has grown well beyond the 4% level within a 25-stock portfolio and using the proceeds to add to another holding that has fallen well below its 4% weighting.

Rebalancing does not have to be absolute and automatic, however. If your reasons for owning a stock remain intact, and its price remains well below what you feel the company is worth, why would you want to sell any of it? Instead of blindly following a process that typically leads to large numbers of tiny, frequent, unnecessary, and potentially costly transactions, I suggest you take this more rational approach to rebalancing your portfolio:

1. Always keep the Reserve account at 30% of your annual gross income. If it drops below that level, divert all of your regular savings deposits into it until the Reserve requirement is satisfied. Once it is, savings deposits should once again be added to the Equity portfolio.

2. Consider selling a portion of any stock position that is more than 20% above its normal weighting within the Equity portfolio. For example, if you hold 25 stocks, then each would normally represent 4% of the total. When any position exceeds 4.8% of the Equity portfolio (4% x 120%), consider reducing it, assuming it no longer represents a compelling bargain. It's your choice whether to sell just enough shares to bring the position below 4.8%, or to take it all the way back down to a standard 4% weighting.

3. Use the proceeds of this sale, along with your regular savings deposits and any dividend income you have received, to add to any of your other holdings that have fallen more than 20% below their 4% weightings (3.2% or less) assuming they represent better opportunities than whatever stocks you are selling.

You should now understand how to build and manage your Equity portfolio, a diversified collection of profitable, well-run businesses dedicated to rewarding you with rising streams of dividend income. Use those dividends to experience the wealth-building wonders of compounding until your portfolio income reaches the point at which—when added to any Social Security and pension benefits you've earned—it can support a lifestyle of your choosing.

That's the day you will be able to stop working for money, or to keep working just because you want to. Many people never have the luxury of making a decision like that.

You now have the nuts and bolts of the True Wealth process. You understand the key principles on which it is based. You know how to build and manage a wealth-building portfolio using the Dividend Method. Keep on earning, saving, investing, dollar-cost averaging, and compounding. You are on the road to True Wealth, and it's time to start watching for mileposts along your way.

SIGNS OF PROGRESS

It's important to stop and make note of the progress you are making along your journey to True Wealth in order to help you keep track of your progress, to provide you with a series of new goals to pursue, and to keep you motivated.

In a later chapter you will find a series of more detailed mileposts based on the number of years you plan to work, but here's a peek at some of the major achievements you will make along the way:

- In the early stages of your journey, you will start seeing steady increases in your savings level, thanks to your monthly deposits, first from digging and filling your financial moat, and then through your investment program as you begin the wealth-building process. The number of shares you own will grow with each new investment, and you will experience the miracle of compounding when you track the number of shares you are accumulating through reinvesting your dividends.

- On the liabilities side of your ledger, you should start noticing a steady decline in your debt level. You'll celebrate when your initial debt target—that first credit card or charge account you decide to pay off—shows a zero balance, and you will be even more motivated to move on to the next one. Add up what you're paying in finance charges each month and watch that number get smaller and smaller over time. By increasing your assets and decreasing your liabilities simultaneously, your net worth should begin to grow doubly quick.

- As your Equity portfolio increases in size, you will start experiencing the volatility that comes along with equity investing. Eventually, in fact, there will be months when the value of your portfolio goes up or down by more than the amount of the deposit you make that month. This might be a little unsettling at first, but it's something you will learn to get used to. We have talked about the power money has to earn even more money, and sooner or later, compounding and volatility will have a greater impact on your month-end balances than what you save. And that's a good thing; it means your money is working harder than you are.

- Watch for the day that the value of your Equity account exceeds what's in your Reserve account. It's an important milepost to reach, and with any luck it will stay that way for the rest of your life.

- Later, celebrate the month that the total value of your portfolio exceeds your annual salary. That's a full year's pay you wouldn't have if you weren't saving, and it will come from *your* efforts, magnified by the magic of compounding.

- You should also be routinely tracking the amount of *income* that your portfolio generates, even though it will be a very tiny number at first and even though it might be decades before you plan to spend any of it. Look at every monthly statement and record the total of all dividends and interest you receive. This number will vary month to month, because companies pay dividends on different cycles throughout the year. But at some point, you will be able to start making *year-over-year* comparisons, and you'll probably like what you see. The income that your portfolio generates will almost certainly be steadier and more consistent than the value of the portfolio itself, because as you know, prices are much more volatile than dividends historically. That's also a good thing.

I can think of three more very good reasons to track your portfolio income regularly. First, it will help you remember that this is income that you didn't have to get up and go to work for. Your *money* is doing more and more of the work now, which might allow *you* to stop working one day if you choose.

Second, this portfolio income number will help you calculate—anytime you want—how close you are to reaching True Wealth. Could you afford to live on this income after adding in Social Security and pensions? If not, how soon could you realistically see that happening?

And third, you will find it reassuring to focus on income instead of prices during challenging markets. It will take your mind off the stresses of the moment, while reminding you that market pullbacks give you the opportunity to reinvest that income into even more shares at lower prices.

TAKEAWAYS:

- Investing in companies that pay rising dividends is a key to attaining True Wealth.

- The Dividend Method allows you to earn dividends today that can be used to purchase additional shares. And if your companies continue increasing their dividends, you'll have even more money to reinvest in the future. It's like compounding within compounding.

- A diversified portfolio includes holdings across several sectors, limiting each sector to no more than 30% of your total Equity portfolio.

- You should research candidates for your Equity portfolio on the basis of quality, financial strength, growth, dividend sustainability, current yield, and value.

- Continue your research to look for new stocks to buy, where to invest future deposits and dividend income, and when to replace or rebalance your current holdings.

- Monitor your progress by keeping track of the dividends your portfolio is generating and how fast that income is increasing over time. It's often more reassuring—and more productive—than watching the markets.

CHAPTER 8

APPROACHING TRUE WEALTH

rue Wealth is the point in life at which you no longer need to work for money.

The nice thing about this definition of wealth is that *you* get to do the defining. *You* have the freedom to determine how much it will cost each year to support the lifestyle *you* have chosen. If you've been tracking the income that your portfolio is generating each year, and you have a good estimate of the Social Security and/or pension benefits you can expect, then at some point the finish line will start coming into view. You will get a better and better idea of how close you are to True Wealth and when you will likely arrive at your destination.

This book is based on the premise that True Wealth is attainable at any income level, because your spending goals will likely be comparable to what you've been spending during your working years. For example, if you want to maintain your current lifestyle after you stop working, you'll need to replace most if not all of the income you've been accustomed to receiving. It will simply be coming from different sources in the future.

It's certainly possible that you envision a simpler, more modest, less expensive way to live once you stop working. If so, you might find yourself reaching the promised land sooner than others. On the other hand, you might be setting your sights on an even richer existence in the future. If that's your goal, you'll likely need to work longer, save more, and grow a larger nest egg to support that lifestyle in retirement. *This is your choice, remember?*

THE TRANSITION TO TRUE WEALTH

Because we don't have the space here to envision every possible scenario, we are going to proceed on the assumption that you want to maintain your current lifestyle once you stop working, which means that you want to continue spending at current levels. The specific mileposts I've created in this chapter are based on this assumption, and you should adapt them to your own definition of True Wealth.

Up to this point, you have been focused on *creating* wealth by (1) setting aside the equivalent of 30% of your annual gross income in a low-risk, liquid Reserve account for emergencies; (2) building a diversi-fied portfolio of 25 rising-dividend companies that meet the Dividend Method standards; and (3) reinvesting all of the income the portfolio generates. As you approach True Wealth, however, your attention will turn to *preserving* wealth and enjoying the rising stream of dividend income you have engineered.

To make this transition a smooth one, I recommend you begin making annual adjustments to your financial life and your portfolio beginning about **five years** before you plan to stop working. In prepara-tion, I'm going to ask you to start thinking about something that will not only play a role in how soon you reach True Wealth but how you maintain it for the rest of your life.

There are two basic approaches to withdrawing money from your portfolio, and you will need to decide which better suits your needs and preferences. You can change your mind along the way, but switching from one method to the other will require substantial adjustments to your plan. And the closer you are to retirement, the bigger those adjustments will need to be.

We will discuss both methods in detail later, but for now let's imagine two different scenarios.

Bob and Mary Smith have three children and seven (soon to be eight) grandchildren. While their large family is doing well financially, they want to make sure that the wealth the two of them have accumulated can be used to care for future generations and some special causes they feel deeply about.

Their plan is to use the income their investments produce to supplement the pensions and Social Security they will receive, while keeping their nest egg largely intact. The *Conserve* approach—which follows the underlying principles of this book—gives them the opportunity to do that. To make it work, the Smiths' portfolio will need to be large enough to generate the income they need without repeatedly dipping into their principal.

Tom and Susan Jones are in a different situation. Their goal is to retire early and spend the rest of their lives traveling the world. They will also need to withdraw from their savings to supplement Social Security, but with no immediate family, they plan to spend as much of their nest egg as possible without depleting it prematurely. The *Consume* approach—which involves systematically "spending down" their portfolio over time—should work better for their situation.

Assuming both couples want to withdraw the same amount of money from their investments to support their chosen lifestyles, it's clear that the Smiths will need to have more money at retirement, because they plan to spend only the income it generates. They will also need to be attentive to how much that cash flow increases over time to stay ahead of inflation.

The Joneses, on the other hand, won't likely need as much money as the Smiths to retire comfortably. With no intention of leaving an inheritance, they will be able to spend the income their portfolio generates *and* consume some of the principal each year. Their biggest concern will be not spending it too quickly, which will require a special strategy and the discipline to follow it for the rest of their lives.

You don't need to settle on a method right now, but it's important to think this through well before you begin your five-year transition to True Wealth.

While you are building wealth, your Reserve account continues to act as a financial cushion against unexpected, temporary setbacks that might make your job more difficult, if not impossible. During the transition to wealth preservation, you will gradually make your financial moat wider and deeper to act as an even more substantial buffer once you stop working.

When that day arrives, you will need money to replace what you've been earning from your job. Some of it will eventually come from Social Security and/or pensions; the rest will come from your investments. *Everything you withdraw from your portfolio will come out of the Reserve account* which, ideally, should be systematically replenished with dividends from the Equity account. This should lessen the need to sell stocks to meet your spending needs.

The objective of the five-year transition is to build up the Reserve account to cover all of the withdrawals you plan to make in the first years of retirement. To accomplish this, you will be shifting funds from your Equity portfolio to the Reserve portfolio each year. Spreading these transfers over five years will help reduce the risk of unfortunate timing.

By the time you're done, you'll have at least enough money "escrowed" in the Reserve account to cover your first five years of planned spending. From that point forward, all of the dividends generated in your Equity portfolio will be added to the Reserve to help replenish what you're spending.

Now, let's map out the five-year transition to True Wealth, one year at a time.

TW MINUS 5: Five Years from True Wealth

You are five years away from your target date. Five years from being financially able to quit working for money. Five years from True Wealth. That might sound like a long time, but you've got a lot to do, and you need to get busy.

Here is what you need to be thinking about now—and doing over the next 12 months:

✓ Continue adding all new savings deposits to your Equity holdings throughout the year and keep reinvesting any dividends you receive along with it.

✓ Choose between the Conserve method and the Consume method. Do you want a portfolio that can fund your chosen lifestyle for the rest of your life—*and* possibly those who live on after you? Or do you want to utilize most of the wealth you've spent a lifetime accumulating, gradually spending it down?

✓ Come up with an estimate—as detailed as you can make it—of what you plan to spend in the first year after you stop working. If you plan to draw Social Security and/or pension benefits by then, you can reduce your total spending goal by those amounts. Make this a *gross* number that includes federal and state income taxes. We have consistently used gross (pretax) income numbers throughout this book, both as it relates to your spending goals and to the idea of maintaining your chosen lifestyle after you stop working. It might be difficult to estimate what tax rate you'll be paying once you're no longer receiving a paycheck, but if you keep it roughly the same as during your working years, you're more likely to err on the conservative side. You will have time to fine-tune these estimates after you have a better idea of your actual expenses.

✓ Once you know how much you will need to withdraw from your investments to cover expenses for your first year of financial independence, **move this amount from the Equity side of your portfolio to the Reserve side.** This will involve selling shares of stocks—probably a substantial number of shares—without disrupting the overall balance of your Equity portfolio. This also represents a good opportunity to get each of your 25 stocks closer to equal weightings by selling from your largest holdings first.

✓ Invest the proceeds from these sales—equal to the full amount of what you plan to withdraw in Year 1 of your retirement—in a fixed-income security with a five-year targeted maturity. It could be a five-year certificate of deposit, or an exchange-traded fund that holds high-quality bonds that mature in five years. *It's important that this be a savings or investment vehicle with a stated maturity.* You need to know exactly when you will have access to this money—and how much it should be worth—when you need it to fund your first year of retirement five years down the road.

✓ You will be repeating this process every year during your five-year transition to True Wealth, and each year you should have a better idea of what your portfolio will look like when you're done. Think ahead and make a conservative estimate of how much your Equity portfolio might be generating in dividend income after five years of these changes. If for whatever reason your estimates come up short, go back and rework the numbers. And if they still don't add up, consider pushing your plans back a year.

✓ If you are married or have a partner, start having some serious discussions about what you both want life to look like when you're no longer going to work every day. Where do you want to live? How will you spend your time? What will it cost to do the big, fun things you've always dreamed of doing? It's important for you both to be on the same page when it comes to your aspirations and expectations. Keep talking about it and design a lifestyle that you both will fully enjoy.

✓ Meet with a qualified financial and tax advisor to begin working on strategies to minimize future taxes. Use this five-year transition period to educate yourself on Roth IRA conversions, required minimum distributions, and Social Security claiming strategies. Get some sound financial and tax advice from professionals you trust and take advantage of their expertise.

TW MINUS 4: Four Years from True Wealth

At four years from your target date, this year's plan looks very similar to TW Minus 5. Here's what you will be focusing on over the next 12 months:

✓ Update your spending estimates for the first two years of retirement. Are they still realistic? Update and sharpen them as necessary.

✓ Make a new conservative projection of what your portfolio will look like four years from now. Remember that you will be shifting money from the Equity side to the Reserve annually for four more years, and you need to feel confident that once those transfers are complete that your annual dividends will come reasonably close to funding a normal year of retirement. If you feel behind schedule for any reason, increase your savings now to compensate or adjust your countdown.

✓ Continue adding all new savings deposits to your Equity holdings and keep reinvesting all dividends there.

✓ Estimate what you expect to withdraw from your portfolio five years from now for your second year of financial independence. Adjust this figure for any Social Security and/or pensions you'll be receiving.

✓ Liquidate this amount now from your Equity portfolio while trying to maintain roughly equal weights in each of your 25 companies.

✓ Use the proceeds of your stock sales to buy another CD or high-quality fixed-income ETF with a target maturity of five years. Do not add it to the investment you chose last year, which should now be four years from its targeted maturity. You want a new CD or fund that will mature in five years, because this is the money you will be withdrawing from your Reserve five years from now to cover your expenses in Year 2 of retirement. In essence, you are building a fixed-income "ladder."

✓ Start learning more about Social Security this year. Read a book, attend a workshop, or ask your financial advisor for information resources. You'll find a wealth of information to get you started on the Social Security Administration web site (ssa.gov), and most of it is written in simple, understandable language.

✓ Start making some decisions about where you will live once you stop working. Many people choose to downsize at this point in life to a smaller, less expensive, more manageable home once the kids are on their own. If you plan to remain in your current home, start budgeting for any big repairs and renovations you expect to make, and make every effort to pay for them out of your current income instead of from your savings.

✓ Begin researching health-care options once you leave work. Will you be able to maintain any coverage through your employer in retirement? And if you stop working before qualifying for Medicare, what options are there for plugging the health-care gap for both you and your spouse? Private health insurance can be expensive, and you will need an ironclad coverage plan in place well before you stop working.

TW MINUS 3: Three Years from True Wealth

It's coming into sharper focus now—this bold idea that you will soon have the option of no longer working for a living, that it's possible to replace your current income with other sources and live the life you've designed. Imagine doing whatever you choose to do with your time from then on—because you can afford to.

To help make it happen, do the following over the next 12 months:

✓ Review your spending projections for Years 1, 2, and 3 of retirement. Update prior estimates for each year as necessary.

✓ At two years into this five-year transition, you should now be getting a much better idea of how your portfolio will look at the end of it. Will your Equity portfolio be able to deliver the income you'll need to help cover expenses—even after moving sizable portions of it into your Reserve account each year for five years? These final years of your working life might offer opportunities to sock away even more money, since the expenses of raising a family and paying off debt should be mostly behind you now. Save as much as you can this year—while you still can.

✓ Add all new savings deposits to your Equity holdings and keep reinvesting the dividends they generate. And if the equity market should decline during the final few years of your career—thank your lucky stars! Keep adding on shares of your favorite companies at discount prices.

✓ It's now time to plan five years ahead to your *third* year of retirement. What do you plan to withdraw from your portfolio in Year 3 to supplement any Social Security and/or pension income you'll be receiving?

✓ Keeping roughly the same amount of dollars in each of your 25 Equity holdings, liquidate enough shares to escrow your planned portfolio withdrawals for Year 3.

✓ Invest the proceeds of these transactions in a fixed-income security—another CD or ETF with a *five-year* targeted maturity.
Once you do this, you should have money maturing in each of
the first *three* years after you stop working. By investing these
funds conservatively, that money is more likely to be there when
you need it, in amounts that you know in advance. Your Reserve
income ladder now has three rungs, *in addition to* the original
amount you've been holding there for emergencies all these years.

✓ This is the year to thoroughly research your pension options from
work and start understanding your payout options. Work with
your financial advisor to decide if it's better to choose a lifetime
monthly payment option—which could also provide an income
for your surviving spouse—or to take your pension benefits as a
lump sum, if available.

✓ Also talk with your employer to see what other benefits you might
qualify for after you leave your job, such as health-care coverage,
life insurance, legal advice, and so on. You don't need to decide
now; just find out what your options will be in retirement.

✓ It's also time to meet with an estate attorney to start planning
your financial legacy if you haven't already. With the attorney's
advice, make sure all of your accounts are properly titled and
that you've designated beneficiaries for all retirement and insurance plans.

TW MINUS 2: Two Years from True Wealth

By this point, True Wealth should be clearly in sight and almost within
your grasp. But remember, this is a *plan*, and the nice thing about it
is that you're the one doing the planning. That means you can adjust
it—and the timetable for making it happen—at your discretion. If you
need extra time to get where you want to be, take it.

And if you *are* right on schedule, here's what you need to be focusing on with just two years to go:

✓ Make sure you're feeling confident about how much money you'll be spending each year after you stop working, and that includes any big onetime expenses that aren't part of your normal monthly plan during the first five years. Set aside money for major trips, home renovation projects, new cars—things that don't happen every year. Anything over and above your normal spending goals for the first five years of retirement should be figured into your plan, earmarked for the specific year(s) you intend to need it.

✓ This is also the time to move enough money from the Equity side of your portfolio to the Reserve side to cover your *fourth* year of retirement withdrawals. Again, keeping the Equity portfolio well-balanced among your 25 holdings, use the proceeds of your share sales to purchase another fixed-income security with a target maturity of *five years*. You are adding the *fourth* step of your five-year fixed-income ladder, and you'll be done building it a year from now.

✓ Keep saving money—and if you can afford to squirrel away any extra, you won't regret it later. Put those deposits—and all the dividend income you're earning—where you see the best opportunities each month among your Equity holdings.

✓ You should be close to paying off all of your debts about now, with a goal of zero debt by the time you stop working. If you're behind schedule on the liability side of the ledger, tighten your belt a little and see if you can pay everything off over these next two years.

✓ Finally, spend more time this year deciding how you will spend your time once you stop working. Many of the clients I work with come to realize that there are just so many rounds of golf they feel like playing each week, just so many fish they feel like catching. Some of them enjoy working part-time or even starting their own businesses—not because they need the money, but because the work gives them a reason to get up in the morning, a purpose. If that sounds like you, consider getting those plans lined up over these next two years.

TW MINUS 1: One Year from True Wealth

Now it's crunch time. Unless you need to make some serious late adjustments, you are just one year away from never having to work for money again. You're just 12 months from financial freedom. True Wealth could be just one more trip around the sun.

Assuming everything is on schedule, here are the tasks you need to check off in your final year as a working-for-money person:

✓ Make a final decision on whether you plan to *conserve* the nest egg you have accumulated through a lifetime of saving, *investing*, and compounding—or *consume* it. Read more about the Conserve and Consume methods in the next chapter and decide which is better suited to what you want to accomplish.

✓ Fine-tune your spending goal for next year, which will be your *first* year of True Wealth. You should have a very specific number in mind by now, but it will still be just an educated guess. As much as you think and plan, you can't know precisely what it will cost to live once you stop working. That does not relieve you of the responsibility of making a conservative good-faith estimate, however.

✓ Just as you have done in each of the last four years, estimate how much money you will need to withdraw from your portfolio to fund your spending needs in Year 5 of retirement.

Systematically sell shares totaling that amount from your Equity portfolio while keeping your holdings in proper balance. Use the proceeds of these sales to purchase a CD or ETF with a target maturity of five years from now. Once you do this, you should have your *first* five years of planned withdrawals "escrowed" in fixed-income securities, and your five-year "ladder" will be complete. By the way, you'll be happy to know that this is the last time you will need to liquidate a significant portion of your Equity portfolio in order to make these transfers. Once you reach True Wealth, the dividends your stocks produce are designed to go toward replacing the fifth rung of your ladder each year.

✓ Continue saving money from each paycheck this year, adding it to your Equity portfolio as you see opportunities. If you choose to stop working once you reach True Wealth, this might also be the last year you'll be saving a big chunk of your income. Take advantage of *any* opportunity—bonuses, overtime, retirement incentives, self-employment income—to save extra.

✓ Meet with a human resources representative at your employer to arrange any retirement benefits you might have earned. Find out what you will receive, in what amounts, and for how long—and get everything in writing.

✓ Decide when and how you will receive any pension benefits you have earned. Do the same for Social Security retirement benefits. Make sure you and your spouse/partner agree on a strategy to maximize your combined retirement benefits.

✓ Get answers to all of your questions about Medicare. If you plan to stop working before Medicare eligibility, make certain your health insurance needs are covered adequately by some other means. Coordinate any retiree health-care benefits with Medicare and purchase supplemental coverage if necessary. You cannot afford to leave yourself or your family vulnerable to major health-care expenses, even for a brief period.

✓ Schedule elective surgeries and dental procedures while you are still employed, even if they will be covered by insurance after you stop working. If any health-related surprises await, it's better to face them while you're still on the job.

THE TRUE WEALTH PORTFOLIO

As you complete your five-year transition into True Wealth, here's a quick summary of what, I believe, your investment portfolio should look like:

Your Reserve portfolio should have enough money to cover planned withdrawals for the next *five years*. Along with any Social Security and pension income you'll be receiving, there should be more than enough in the Reserve to support the lifestyle you have chosen and planned for. That first certificate of deposit or fixed-income ETF that you purchased five years ago should now be approaching maturity, and this cash should satisfy the withdrawals you make over the first 12 months after you leave work.

This process will repeat itself for the next four years, with the systematic maturity and liquidation of the remaining four original rungs of your fixed-income ladder. They were designed to fund portfolio withdrawals for your spending needs for each of the coming years. As a cushion, your Reserve also contains the original "moat"—money that has been there all along for financial emergencies.

Your Equity portfolio strategy has been designed for you to own shares of 25 successful companies—your "business partners"—who pay you regular cash dividends and have the potential to give you "raises" in the future. The total income you receive from dividends each year should roughly equal your annual portfolio spending needs, and you want to see this dividend income increase faster than inflation in most years.

Your job in retirement is to manage and maintain these two investment accounts for the rest of your life. It shouldn't take up too much of your time, which should be welcome news now that you have more interesting ways to spend it.

TAKEAWAYS

- Review the plans for each of the five years before you retire.

- In each of those years, transition a portion of your Equity portfolio into the Reserve portfolio, from which you will draw income in retirement.

- Consider whether you want to Conserve or Consume your investment portfolio.

CHAPTER 9

BEYOND TRUE WEALTH

When you reach the point in your life when you no longer need to work for money, there's a good chance that you will possess greater financial wealth than you ever have before—perhaps even more than you ever *dreamed* of having.

You are now the beneficiary of a lifetime of your own good habits, multiplied by years and years of compounding. Better yet, the very best part of your life—financially and otherwise—might very well lie ahead of you.

But the game isn't over; it's only halftime.

Achieving True Wealth isn't easy, but it can be a straightforward process: Spend less than you earn, invest the difference, and repeat. Once you stop working, however, it gets a bit more complex. The stakes increase once you leave the security of a regular paycheck behind. In fact, it's been said that the two most dangerous days of your life are the day you're born and the day you retire. Both events can be stressful, even life-threatening.

MAKING WEALTH LAST

If you've made it this far, however, you are leagues ahead of most people, simply because you have a plan. You've had one from the day you launched your journey to True Wealth. That plan focused on building wealth, and now you can begin truly enjoying it. But that will require a different kind of plan.

The task ahead of you is twofold: (1) create a dependable stream of income that, along with Social Security and/or pensions, is adequate to support the lifestyle you have chosen, and (2) make sure that income increases over time at least as much as your cost of living.

Many retirees make the mistake of underestimating or even ignoring inflation. They assume that because the biggest purchases of their lives are behind them inflation no longer poses a threat. Sensing a need to "protect their principal" they become more attracted to the lower volatility of short-term fixed-income investments. Many people never learn that inflation, like debt, can compound *against* them for the rest of their lives.

If you think of money as *purchasing power*, then risk is the potential *extinction* of purchasing power. Safety, in those terms, is an ample, dependable *income that consistently rises* faster than one's cost of living. If your expenses are going to keep increasing in retirement, shouldn't your income?

I often ask newly retired clients two questions that seem to help them grasp the threat that inflation poses. The first is: *"What did you pay more for, your last car—or your first house?"* That puts inflation in terms they can instantly relate to.

The second question is: *"Would you take a job that promised you a nice salary for the next 30 years if you knew you would never get a pay raise?"* Of course they wouldn't, and neither would you.

But many new retirees will happily accept a similar offer when it comes to their retirement income. They will forgo the lump sum payout from their pension plans in lieu of a promise of monthly income for life—*with no raises*. They will invest in 30-year government bonds with a guarantee of principal—and *fixed* interest payments. And sometimes they will accept a free steak dinner from someone who wants to sell them a high-cost, high-commission annuity that turns their life's savings into a promise of lifetime income payments—*typically with no increases.*

A retirement income strategy that focuses exclusively on the lower volatility of fixed-income investments is no strategy at all. It's a chimera. Facing two or three decades of rising expenses with an income that never increases is a recipe for disaster, or as author Nick Murray puts it, "suicide on the installment plan."

To sustain True Wealth once you achieve it, your portfolio must generate an income that can increase over time faster than your cost of living, while also maintaining its potential for future appreciation. It's not just about growth anymore. And it's not all about income, either. It's about *growth of income*—now and forevermore.

The dividends that helped you compound wealth during your working years can provide a rising stream of income once you stop working. But now, instead of reinvesting those dividends, you will be spending them—and enjoying them. And to the extent that those dividends might rise *faster* than your living expenses, your options become even more attractive.

THE CONSERVE METHOD

Earlier I mentioned two basic approaches to managing your investment portfolio in retirement. One involves *conserving* wealth by living largely off the income your investments create. The other involves *consuming* your nest egg by carefully spending it down over the remainder of your life.

At face value, neither approach is superior to the other. But depending on your needs and preferences, one will likely better suit your needs.

Under the Conserve method (upon which the thesis of this book is based), you will be making planned spending withdrawals from the Reserve portion of your portfolio each year. During the five-year transition leading up to the day you stop working for money, you systematically and annually transferred money from your Equity portfolio to the Reserve portfolio to "escrow" your spending needs for each of the first five years of retirement.

From this point forward, all of your withdrawals will come from the Reserve, and all of the dividends generated on the Equity side of your portfolio will be invested on the Reserve side to replenish what you are withdrawing each year. Specifically, you will use these dividends to purchase shares of a fixed-income ETF with a targeted *five-year* maturity. In essence, you will be rebuilding the top rung of your five-year fixed-income ladder over the course of each year while spending the proceeds of the bottom rung, which recently matured.

At this point, you could be wondering why the Reserve fund is even necessary any longer. If your dividend income is sufficient to cover your spending needs, why invest them in fixed-income funds for the next five years? Why not just live off the dividends as you receive them?

Three reasons. First, if you have been tracking your dividend income, you have noticed how greatly your cash flow can vary month to month. By withdrawing your spending money in even installments from the Reserve portfolio, you'll be able to set up automatic transfers to your checking account each month to cover your spending needs, as opposed to varying your spending based on the timing of dividend payments. You will know the exact amount of cash to expect each month and when you will receive it, just like when you were working and receiving a regular paycheck.

Second, having a five-year spending cushion in the Reserve gives you, at minimum, the confidence of knowing that you won't need to liquidate shares of stock to cover your living expenses—at least not for the next five years—and possibly forever. It's comforting to know that all of your planned spending needs for the next five years can likely be met without facing the risk of selling stocks at the wrong time.

Third, maintaining the Reserve gives you the flexibility—*as it always has*—to cover large, unexpected expenses that may continue to crop up from time to time. You will replenish the Reserve when you see opportunities in the future.

You might also be wondering what would happen if your Equity portfolio doesn't generate enough in dividends in a given year to cover your planned spending needs five years out. Even though you've been focusing on companies that have the capacity to increase their dividends faster than inflation over time, you admittedly have little control over where current yields happen to be at the time you purchase shares. For that reason, it's not uncommon to come up a little short, especially in the early years of retirement.

It's completely acceptable to liquidate a few shares of your most successful equity investments—or the ones you consider overvalued—from time to time to make up any reasonable dividend shortfall. With time and dividend growth, this will probably become less and less necessary, if indeed it ever is.

What you *don't* want to do with the Conserve method is to make selling shares of stock a long-term or permanent habit in order to cover your spending. If you are consistently spending more than the income you are receiving from Social Security, pensions, and dividends each year, you might want to rethink your spending goals, or perhaps even consider some version of the Consume method, which we will discuss in greater detail later in this chapter.

MANAGING THE CONSERVE PORTFOLIO

How do you manage your portfolio under the Conserve approach? It's a process that begins on the day you stop working for money and continues for the rest of your life:

1. Start tracking what you spend each month and year and keep yourself as much on plan as possible. This is especially important in the first few years of retirement when you are settling into your new lifestyle and spending habits.

2. Having completed the five-year transition period leading up to True Wealth, you should now have enough ready cash in the Reserve account to cover whatever withdrawals you plan to make for the next 12 months, net of any Social Security and pension income you'll be receiving. If you can earn a little interest on this money over the course of the year, that's great. Just keep it in a low-volatility, liquid investment vehicle.

3. The rest of your Reserve portfolio should now be mostly invested in four ETFs or CDs, each with a different target maturity. One should self-liquidate a year from now, another in two years, another in three years, and a final pool of money set to mature four years from now.

4. As you receive dividends from the stocks you own in your Equity portfolio, use them to buy shares in a new ETF, one with a *five-year* target maturity. This money represents the new top rung in your five-year fixed-income ladder, and you should be adding dividend income to it on a monthly basis for the next year.

5. You probably have more time on your hands now, and it's vital that you resist the temptation to overmanage your Equity portfolio. Some of your holdings might amaze you, and others will likely disappoint you, but remember that over time stocks generally tend to reflect how their underlying businesses are faring. That's not to say that you shouldn't replace holdings when you see opportunities; just don't make a new career out of it.

6. Toward the end of each year from now on, make sure there's enough invested in your new five-year fixed-income fund to cover the withdrawals you expect to make five years down the

road. If there's not enough to meet your projected needs, review your Equity holdings and decide where you might trim some shares to make up the shortfall. Assuming your annual spending needs are fairly consistent, and your dividend income is increasing faster than inflation, you probably won't need to sell from the Equity portfolio very often, if at all.

7. At some point in the future, you may discover that your annual dividend income actually *exceeds* what you plan to spend from the portfolio five years from now. If this happens regularly, as it might, you have several nice options: (1) let the extra cash build up in the Reserve account, increasing your cash cushion; (2) keep adding it to the five-year ETF to give you even more to spend five years from now; (3) use it to buy more shares of your favorite Equity holdings and let compounding resume; or (4) target the surplus cash toward a special purpose, such as education expenses, travel, charitable giving, or a long-term health-care reserve.

8. Repeat this process every year, fine-tuning it along the way as your needs and circumstances change.

THE CONSUME METHOD

Early in this book we agreed that you were solely responsible for your financial future and thereby entitled to enjoy all of the successes you achieve. Well, that also includes how you choose to use the wealth you've accumulated through a lifetime of disciplined saving and investing.

In short, *you* get to decide whether to use that wealth to create a legacy for future generations to enjoy—or to *enjoy it yourself* to the fullest extent possible. It's your money. It's your choice.

The Conserve method involves spending the income your portfolio generates to fund a lifestyle that you have chosen, while eventually passing along most if not all of the principal however you choose.

If that's not what you prefer—or don't feel you can afford—there is a second approach: the Consume method. The idea here is to carefully and systematically spend down your portfolio over your retirement years. There is no right or wrong approach. Choose the one that better suits your financial needs and desires.

Naturally, the Consume method allows you to spend more money each year since conserving the principal for future generations is not a concern. It *does* require you to be very disciplined in your spending, however, especially during periods of lower-than-average investment returns, which will occur from time to time.

This approach uses life expectancy tables as a general guideline for determining how much of your portfolio it's reasonable to spend each year. The IRS publishes these tables—and updates them from time to time to reflect changes in overall life expectancy—to set required minimum distribution (RMD) amounts from traditional IRAs, 401(k) plans, and similar tax-deferred retirement accounts once you reach a certain age.

The idea behind RMDs is to require annual distributions from tax-deferred accounts based on the owner's life expectancy so that most of the money in these accounts is withdrawn—and taxed—over his or her lifetime. Life expectancy goes to age 120+ in these tables, which for all intents and purposes means tax-deferred assets are never required to be fully liquidated.

Using that same logic, the RMD tables can also serve as a handy guideline for systematically "consuming" your retirement nest egg—both taxable *and* tax-deferred assets—without running any substantial risk of exhausting it over the course of your life. At the beginning of each year, you will add up the total value of your portfolio—Reserve and Equity combined—and multiply it by the appropriate percentage from the table below based on your age. The result will give you a reasonable idea of how much you can afford to spend over the following 12 months. Then, simply repeat the process each year.

The percentages below were derived using figures from the IRS's

Joint and Last Survivor Table. They assume that you and your spouse are within 10 years in age of each other. If your age difference is greater, you should adjust these figures using the full tables published in IRS Publication 590-B:

Joint Life Expectancy Table		
Age	Divisor	Percentage
50	48.5	2.06%
51	47.5	2.11%
52	46.5	2.15%
53	45.6	2.19%
54	44.6	2.24%
55	43.6	2.29%
56	42.6	2.35%
57	41.6	2.40%
58	40.7	2.46%
59	39.7	2.52%
60	38.7	2.58%
61	37.7	2.65%
62	36.8	2.72%
63	35.8	2.79%
64	34.9	2.87%
65	33.9	2.95%
66	33.0	3.03%
67	32.0	3.13%
68	31.1	3.22%
69	30.1	3.32%
70	29.2	3.42%
71	28.3	3.53%
72	27.4	3.65%
73	26.5	3.77%
74	25.5	3.92%
75	24.6	4.07%
76	23.7	4.22%
77	22.9	4.37%
78	22.0	4.55%

CONTINUED

Joint Life Expectancy Table		
Age	Divisor	Percentage
79	21.1	4.74%
80	20.2	4.95%
81	19.4	5.15%
82	18.5	5.41%
83	17.7	5.65%
84	16.8	5.95%
85	16.0	6.25%
86	15.2	6.58%
87	14.4	6.94%
88	13.7	7.30%
89	12.9	7.75%
90	12.2	8.20%
91	11.5	8.70%
92	10.8	9.26%
93	10.1	9.90%
94	9.5	10.53%
95	8.9	11.24%
96	8.4	11.90%
97	7.8	12.82%
98	7.3	13.70%
99	6.8	14.71%
100	6.4	15.63%

Note that the spending guidelines in the table above are designed for *two lives*. If you are single and planning based on your life only, consider using the table below, which will allow you to withdraw a larger percentage of your portfolio each year while minimizing the risk of exhausting your capital:

Single Life Expectancy Table		
Age	Divisor	Percentage
50	36.2	2.76%
51	35.3	2.83%
52	34.3	2.92%
53	33.4	2.99%
54	32.5	3.08%
55	31.6	3.16%
56	30.6	3.27%
57	29.8	3.36%
58	28.9	3.46%
59	28.0	3.57%
60	27.1	3.69%
61	26.2	3.82%
62	25.4	3.94%
63	24.5	4.08%
64	23.7	4.22%
65	22.9	4.37%
66	22.0	4.55%
67	21.2	4.72%
68	20.4	4.90%
69	19.6	5.10%
70	18.8	5.32%
71	18.0	5.56%
72	17.2	5.81%
73	16.4	6.10%
74	15.6	6.41%
75	14.8	6.76%
76	14.1	7.09%
77	13.3	7.52%
78	12.6	7.94%
79	11.9	8.40%
80	11.2	8.93%
81	10.5	9.52%
82	9.9	10.10%
83	9.3	10.75%
84	8.7	11.49%

CONTINUED

Single Life Expectancy Table		
Age	Divisor	Percentage
85	8.1	12.35%
86	7.6	13.16%
87	7.1	14.08%
88	6.6	15.15%
89	6.1	16.39%
90	5.7	17.54%
91	5.3	18.87%
92	4.9	20.41%
93	4.6	21.71%
94	4.3	23.26%
95	4.0	25.00%
96	3.7	27.03%
97	3.4	29.41%
98	3.2	31.25%
99	3.0	33.33%
100	2.8	35.71%

Again, you should consider these as *general* spending guidelines, and if you choose to follow the Consume method, they might prevent you from withdrawing too much money too soon from your portfolio in retirement. They will also help you recalibrate your annual withdrawals after big changes in your portfolio that may occur after major market swings or unexpected expenses.

MANAGING THE CONSUME PORTFOLIO

With the Consume approach, the goal is to have access to most of your wealth over the rest of your life without fully depleting it. This approach should allow you to spend more than under the Conserve method, but it also means there will likely be less to leave behind when you're gone.

Here is how to manage your portfolio under the Consume method:

- Record what you spend each month and year and keep yourself on track as much as possible. This is especially important in the first few years of retirement when you are settling into your new lifestyle and spending habits.

- Use one of the tables above to determine how much you can reasonably withdraw from your portfolio in Year 1 of your retirement, based on your age and the size of your nest egg. If you and your spouse/partner are separated in age by more than 10 years, refer to the alternate tables published in IRS Publication 590-B.

- The five-year transition period leading up to True Wealth is essentially the same for both the Conserve and Consume approach. By the time you stop working, you should have enough in cash in the Reserve portfolio to cover your planned portfolio withdrawals for the next 12 months, net of Social Security and pension income. Keep these funds in a low-volatility, liquid investment vehicle.

- In addition to cash to cover your spending in Year 1, the Reserve portfolio should also contain four CDs or fixed-income ETFs with target maturities of one, two, three, and four years.

- Invest all of the dividends you receive from companies in your Equity portfolio in a new ETF with a five-year target maturity. This money represents the top rung in your five-year fixed-income ladder, and you should be adding dividend income to it on a regular basis in the year ahead.

- Keep the five-year ladder intact by following this process; make up any annual shortfalls by selectively selling from the Equity portfolio.

- Continue to look for new opportunities to upgrade your Equity holdings but avoid excessively trading your portfolio.

- As the end of Year 1 approaches, try to get an idea whether there's enough in your five-year ETF to cover your projected expenses for Year 5 of retirement. You don't have to stick the landing here, however. Just make a general approximation, knowing that your annual spending will be guided by the percentages outlined in the tables we discussed.

- Your objectives each year from now on are to: (1) make a good-faith estimate of how much you plan to withdraw from your portfolio over each of the next five years, using the appropriate table from the last section as a general guide; (2) keep these approximate amounts "escrowed" in fixed-income ETFs with targeted maturities spread over that five-year period; and (3) keep your spending in line with the annual percentage guidelines as best you can.

- Repeat this process every year, fine-tuning it along the way.

You might feel for whatever reason that the RMD guidelines limit your spending more than you would prefer, especially in the early years of retirement when you would like to spend more. If you choose to spend more, that's your decision. These guidelines are intended to lessen the risk of spending too much of your savings too soon, and the more closely you follow them, the more likely you'll be able to make your portfolio last for as long as you need it to.

MILEPOSTS

"However beautiful the strategy,
you should occasionally look at the results."
—WINSTON CHURCHILL

True Wealth is based on a very simple premise: By following a series of disciplines—spending less than you earn, eliminating debt, investing for compound returns—you are likely to eventually reach a point at which you can afford to stop working for money. All the money you saved and invested during your working years can keep working just as hard for you, giving you the freedom to spend the rest of your life doing whatever you choose.

This section lays out a series of mileposts to mark your progress. Keep in mind, however, that these are simply mileposts, not deadlines, stepping-stones, not mandates. Perhaps you got a late start and have some catching up to do; these mileposts will help you see how far you've come and what it will take to get where you want to be. And if you're farther along in the journey, they will show you how close you are to your destination.

These are ambitious targets based on realistic return expectations. They're designed to provide you with a comfortable margin of safety once you reach True Wealth. Remember that even if you don't reach the next milepost as soon as you planned, you are still well ahead of where you would be if you hadn't made the effort.

Here are the basic assumptions upon which the mileposts were created:

- A 40-year career. That's four full decades of working, saving, and compounding toward True Wealth. Have less time or want to get there sooner? Adjust your goals and the mileposts to your own needs and desires. No one is telling you how long you must work; it's your plan and your timetable.

- Most people will need to replace about one-half (50%) of their final gross (pretax) income in order to enjoy a similar standard of living in retirement. Here's how that figure was derived:

  » Once you stop working, you will no longer be saving 15% of your gross income each year. You have already been living on 85% of your annual salary at most.

  » You will also no longer be subject to payroll (FICA) taxes on your income, which account for *at least* another 5% you won't need to spend. That gets us down to 80%.

» The Social Security Administration suggests that its retirement benefits should replace about 40% of the average
American's employment income. The lower your income,
the more of it that Social Security will likely replace, and
at higher income levels the replacement amount could
be lower than the 40% average. Let's be conservative and
assume that Social Security will replace just 30% of your
income once you stop working. That brings us to our
50% number.

» You will notice I'm not assuming any pension benefits.
Defined-benefit plans have become much less common over
the years. If you qualify for one, it might mean that you will
need to replace *even less than 50%* of your gross income to
maintain the same standard of living.

» Many retirees also end up spending less in several areas:
commuting, life and disability insurance premiums, mortgage payments, clothing, and so on. But other costs, such
as health care, often *increase* in retirement. For our purposes we assume these cost increases and decreases will
offset each other, but you may have to adjust them to your
own situation.

As you look through the following mileposts, try to keep the definition of True Wealth front of mind. If you are able to stop working
one day and have all of your future spending needs met from alternate
income sources, you've succeeded. Whether that income is from pensions, Social Security, rental property, stock dividends, or anyplace
else isn't nearly as important as knowing that it will be reliable, sufficient for your needs, consistent, and able to increase over time at
least as much as what it costs to live the way you want to live for the
rest of your life.

MILEPOST: 40 Years from True Wealth

✓ As you begin your journey, carefully track every dollar you spend for the next 90 days, noting any ways you might be able to reduce your spending in the future.

✓ Start saving 15% of every dollar you earn in a low-volatility, liquid emergency reserve account.

✓ Assess your current debt situation. If you owe money other than a mortgage, set aside an additional 5% of your gross income and launch the seven-step debt elimination plan right away. Aim for a debt-to-income (DTI) ratio no higher than 40.

✓ Set up a spending plan that will enable you to live on 85% of your income (80% if you have nonmortgage debt). Focus on one spending category at a time.

✓ Keep adding to your emergency reserve until it reaches the equivalent of 30% of your annual gross (pretax) income. This should take you less than two years.

✓ Once your moat is complete, start investing in a 401(k) or similar retirement plan at work. Contribute at least enough to qualify for any matching contribution your employer offers. Invest for long-term growth.

✓ Get a complete understanding of every employee benefit available to you—health insurance, flexible spending accounts, education, skills training, and so on—and take full advantage of them. Invest in yourself.

MILEPOST: 35 Years from True Wealth

✓ Maintain an emergency reserve equal to 30% of your annual gross (pretax) income.

✓ Fund a Roth IRA while your income is still below the annual contribution limits. If you already make too much to fund a Roth, see if your employer's retirement plan offers a Roth option. Keep investing your retirement assets for long-term growth.

✓ If you have any self-employment income, explore a Simplified Employee Pension (SEP) IRA as an additional tax-advantaged way to save for retirement.

✓ If you are married and one spouse stops working to take care of a child or for any other reason, fund a spousal IRA or Roth IRA each year.

✓ Pay off all of your credit card debt and pay balances in full each month from now on.

✓ **Portfolio income milepost**: Calculate the total amount of annual income your portfolio is producing. It should be roughly the equivalent of **1.2% of your gross income** each year.

✓ **Savings milepost**: Your nest egg should total around **0.8 times your annual gross income** (80%) at this point. (*Note*: The savings mileposts are rough estimates designed to give you another way to measure your progress over time. It's likely that your portfolio value will fluctuate greatly around these benchmarks, and they are far less important to your success than the income your investments are designed to generate each year.)

✓ **Debt milepost**: Your debt-to-income (DTI) ratio should be **35 or below**.

MILEPOST: 30 Years from True Wealth

✓ Maintain an emergency reserve equal to 30% of your annual gross (pretax) income. You may need to add to it periodically as your income grows. And if you ever have to tap into these funds, make refilling the moat your priority.

✓ As your income and assets increase, insuring them against financial disaster becomes a priority, especially if you have a family depending on you. Life insurance can help replace your income if you die prematurely, and it should still be relatively inexpensive at this point in your life. The greater risk right now is disability, and you must have a plan in place to keep a portion of your income coming in if you're unable to work. See what's available through your employer, and research other options if you need more coverage.

✓ Meet with an attorney to create a will and other estate planning documents. At a minimum, name guardians for your minor children if something were to happen to you and your spouse.

✓ **Portfolio income milepost:** The total income your portfolio generates each year should be equal to approximately **4% of your annual gross income.**

✓ **Savings milepost:** Total savings and investments should be about **2 times your annual gross income.**

✓ **Debt milepost:** Your debt-to-income (DTI) ratio should be at **30 or below,** and you should be paying off your credit cards routinely every month.

MILEPOST: 25 Years from True Wealth

✓ Maintain your emergency reserve at the equivalent of 30% of your annual gross income.

✓ You might be entering your 40s about now, so saving money should be getting easier for you, especially if you have eliminated your nonmortgage debts. Now look at the average annual increase in your portfolio (in dollars) over the past few years. It might be a pleasant surprise when you see the total increase exceeding the amount you're adding to your savings in some years. This means your money is beginning to work harder than you are!

✓ If you're hitting your stride now in terms of earned income and being pushed into higher tax brackets, you'll want to find productive ways to pay less. Meet with a qualified tax advisor and develop a long-term strategy. However, remember that the only thing worse than having to pay taxes is to earn so little that you don't *have* to pay them. Taxes are the price of financial success and one of the ways you contribute to society, but that doesn't mean you should pay more than you are required to.

✓ **Portfolio income milepost:** Each year your portfolio should be generating the rough equivalent of **8% of your annual gross income.** Keep reinvesting that money.

✓ **Savings milepost:** Your total portfolio value should equal at least **3 times your annual gross income.**

✓ **Debt milepost:** Your debt-to-income (DTI) ratio should be **25 or below.**

MILEPOST: 20 Years from True Wealth

✓ Keep the emergency reserve equal to 30% of your annual gross income.

✓ At this point you should see your hard work paying off and producing tangible results. Compounding is working its magic, and money is a willing partner working alongside you, helping you toward your goals. You're still rolling the rock uphill, but somehow the hill doesn't seem quite as steep as it used to.

✓ Look for opportunities to save more, catching up some if you need to. This should be easier once your nonmortgage debts are paid off. You can then redirect that extra 5% of your annual income toward other goals, if you choose, such as education savings plans for your children, a nicer home, or perhaps even an investment property.

✓ If you are saving for college, don't let this or any other objective take priority over your own goal of financial independence. As much you might prefer to avoid it, you can always borrow for college, but you can't borrow your way to True Wealth.

✓ **Portfolio income milepost:** Your annual portfolio income should be running at the equivalent of about **13% of your annual gross income.**

✓ **Savings milepost:** Your total portfolio value should be about **5 times your annual gross income.**

✓ **Debt milepost:** Your debt-to-income (DTI) ratio should be **20 or below.**

MILEPOST: 15 Years from True Wealth

✓ Maintain the equivalent of 30% of your annual gross income in a conservative, liquid savings vehicle.

✓ Familiarize yourself with any pension options you have through your employer.

✓ Set up an online account at the Social Security Administration and start learning how the system works. If you spot any discrepancies in your earnings record, get them corrected as soon as possible.

✓ **Portfolio income milepost:** Your annual portfolio income should be the equivalent of about **20% of your annual gross income.**

Use this cash to buy more shares of your favorite equity holdings where you see opportunities, which should be designed to create even greater income in the future.

✓ **Savings milepost:** Your portfolio value should be at least **7 times your annual gross income.**

✓ **Debt milepost:** Your debt-to-income (DTI) ratio should be **15 or below.**

MILEPOST: 10 Years from True Wealth

✓ This is the get-real decade. Check your progress toward True Wealth, not just with these mileposts but against your own personal deadlines. Can you visualize the finish line?

✓ Keep your emergency reserve equivalent to 30% of your annual gross income.

✓ If you are age 50 or older, take advantage of catch-up contributions to add more to your retirement savings through IRAs and employer plans.

✓ Fully fund a health savings account (HSA) if you qualify. It could become a valuable income source after you stop working.

✓ Have a qualified attorney draft a comprehensive estate plan for you and your spouse and make certain your beneficiary designations are accurate and complete. Start thinking about the legacy you want to leave your loved ones, financial and otherwise.

✓ Start paying a little extra on your mortgage if you haven't already, with a goal of being 100% debt free by the time you stop working.

✓ Think about what you want your life to look like once you can do what you want. Have a heart to heart with your spouse to make sure your dreams are compatible and affordable.

✓ **Portfolio income milepost:** Your annual portfolio income should be running at the equivalent of about **28% of your annual gross income.**

✓ **Savings milepost:** Your portfolio value should be more than **10 times your annual gross income.**

✓ **Debt milepost:** Your debt-to-income (DTI) ratio should be at **10 or below.**

MILEPOST: 5 Years from True Wealth

✓ Crunch time. Take advantage of every opportunity to squirrel away extra savings. You and your spouse should have some concrete ideas by this point on what life will look like—and how much it could change—five years from now.

✓ Launch the five-year transition process described in Chapter 8. Each year, transfer the equivalent of one year's living expenses (net of any other income you will receive) from your Equity portfolio into the Reserve. Repeat this process for the next five years.

✓ Research your Social Security and pension options fully and start narrowing in on a claiming strategy that will maximize your retirement income benefits over both your and your spouse's lives.

✓ Prepare to enroll in Medicare at age 65. Coordinate it with any retirement health-care benefits you expect to receive from your employer.

✓ Consider establishing a home equity line of credit (HELOC) as a source of emergency funds in retirement, though this might not be for everyone. It will be easier to get this in place while you are still working and able to document earned income.

✓ **Portfolio income milepost:** Your annual portfolio income should be about the equivalent of **40% of your annual gross income.**

Use this cash to buy more shares of your favorite equity holdings where you see opportunities.

✓ **Savings milepost:** Your total portfolio value should be around **15 times your annual gross income.**

✓ **Debt milepost:** Your debt-to-income (DTI) ratio should be **5 or below.** Bear down on your mortgage if you haven't paid it off already.

MILEPOST: Arriving at True Wealth

✓ Complete the five-year transition process into True Wealth. Your next five years of planned portfolio withdrawals—to cover the *first* five years of your retirement—should now be escrowed in the Reserve portfolio with maturities targeted to each of those years.

✓ Select a strategy for claiming Social Security benefits coordinated with your spouse.

✓ Enroll in Medicare at age 65 and have a plan in place to cover medical expenses that Medicare doesn't.

✓ Once your retirement income sources are in place, reassess your insurance needs. You might not need as much life insurance, if any. Disability insurance will likely no longer apply to you. Revisit your homeowners, auto, and general liability insurance coverage to make sure you have what you need on the most attractive terms. Get some advice from a qualified insurance professional.

✓ If you own your home, do some preliminary research on reverse mortgages as a fallback source of retirement income. This is not appropriate for everyone, however, and should require extensive research if suitable. If all goes according to plan you won't need it, but your home equity can be a valuable resource if you ever need to tap it as a last line of defense.

✓ Have a comprehensive estate plan in place and discuss it with your family on a regular basis. Review it with your estate attorney every five years or so and fine-tune it as necessary.

✓ **Portfolio income milepost:** Your annual portfolio income should be equivalent to about **50% of your final salary.** Of course, the true test is whether this income—supplemented by pension and Social Security benefits—is enough to support the lifestyle you and your spouse have chosen for the rest of your lives.

✓ **Savings milepost:** Your portfolio value should be close to **20 times your annual gross income.**

✓ **Debt milepost:** Your debt-to-income (DTI) ratio should be **zero.** And you should remain debt free for the rest of your long life.

✓ Book a trip with your spouse to celebrate reaching True Wealth. When you get back home, buy a monthly calendar and start filling it up with activities that bring you both joy. If you have chosen to stop working, be sure you are retiring *to* something, and not just *from* something.

CHAPTER 10

CREATING YOUR LEGACY

I can't create your legacy for you. Only you can do that. Only you can truly understand what matters most to you in the world when it comes to applying what you've earned—and what you've learned—for the benefit of others. I can't tell you what you should do with your fortune once it has served its purpose for you.

But I might be able to give you a few ideas.

Regardless of the financial legacy you choose to leave, the wealth you have created for yourself through a lifetime of effort, wisdom, and experience comes with an unspoken obligation to pass along what you have *learned*. And if you meet that obligation, it could mean more to the people you love than any sum of money you could ever bestow upon them.

Your money can live on after you are gone. With proper guidance, it will keep on working for others just as hard as it has worked for you, and it can provide them financial security and confidence that relatively few people could ever dream of.

More important than money, however, the *wisdom* you have acquired over your lifetime can also be passed along to the people and institutions you care about. And in that sense, you never completely leave them.

> "The first step in the acquisition of wisdom is silence.
> The second, listening.
> The third, memory.
> The fourth, practice.
> The fifth, teaching others."
> —SOLOMON IBN GABIROL

YOUR LEGACY OF WEALTH

If you have understood the three key concepts of this book, have followed its guiding principles while avoiding common temptations, and had the patience and discipline to carry out its simple instructions, it's likely that you will possess more wealth than at any point in your life when you stop working for money.

That's especially the case if you choose to follow the Conserve method, which aims for a stream of income that exceeds your steadily rising cost of living, while allowing you to pass along your wealth to the people and causes you care about. And even if you choose to consume most of your accumulated wealth throughout your retirement, there may still be a sizable sum that you will never need or desire to spend.

With your own financial needs met, you have some enticing options that will allow others to live better lives as a result of your efforts long after you're gone. Let me offer a few examples:

- Pass your wealth along to family members, who can reinvest and compound the dividends until they need the cash flow to fund their own retirements.

- Leave your portfolio to your children, with the condition that the income it generates be used for a specific purpose, such as funding college tuition for your grandchildren—and *their* children.

- Endow a scholarship fund that will make higher education possible for other deserving but less fortunate students.

- Fund a trust to provide lifelong care and support for family members with special needs.

- Set up a charitable trust that will allow you to enjoy the income your investments produce, while leaving the remainder of the portfolio to important causes that you support.

- Create a family foundation to support charities, nonprofits, schoolteachers, medical research organizations, or something else you care deeply about. Put your adult children in charge of running the foundation and making annual grants. They will see firsthand the power of money to do good.

The possibilities your legacy creates are limited only by your imagination. What I want you to understand—regardless of where you are now on the path to True Wealth—is that all of the learning and working and saving and investing and planning that you've been doing will not only help satisfy your own needs during your time on earth. It can also endow future generations and charitable causes with greater financial security.

This little project of yours never has to stop.

"We make a living by what we get. We make a life by what we give."
—WINSTON CHURCHILL

YOUR LEGACY OF WISDOM

As you reach the later stages of your life, you might find yourself in possession of a modest fortune or perhaps even a mighty one. Wealth is relative after all, and what truly matters is whether you ever reach a point where you can afford to stop working for money—and start to enjoy the freedom of deciding exactly how to spend each day of your life.

If you are successful on the journey this book describes, you will one day get to decide what will become of your wealth when you are no longer here. That can mean more than money. Don't discount the value of what you have *learned* along the way. Data yields information, which yields knowledge, which can yield wisdom. And the legacy of wisdom and your experience cannot be overstated.

Some of what you have learned may have come to you the hard way: by committing unforced financial errors, making investment decisions that were questionable in hindsight, or falling prey to your emotions. That's all okay. Teddy Roosevelt once said that the only people who don't make mistakes are the ones who don't do anything.

Undoubtedly, in addition to what experience has taught you, you've picked up some financial wisdom from this book. It is now your moral obligation to share this with those you love.

If I give you a dollar, and then you give me a dollar, neither of us is any better off as a result. But if I give you an *idea*, and then you give me an idea, we both benefit. And if I *teach* you something, and then you teach me something, those benefits can last a lifetime.

Share the principles in these pages with others who respect your opinions and advice. Show them what becomes of the person who accepts full responsibility for his or her actions and the results they produce. Teach them how to live well on less than they earn and to put the difference to work for the future benefit of themselves and others. Help them on their own journey to True Wealth.

Listen. Learn. Remember. Practice. And finally, teach. Others will want to know how you did this and showing them could be the greatest gift they ever receive.

A FINAL THOUGHT

You may have finished reading this book quickly, but if I've done my job, you will be enjoying its benefits for the rest of your life. That is certainly my wish for you.

These words might have found you at the very start of your journey to True Wealth, or perhaps we are meeting somewhere along the path. You might complete the journey or finish somewhere short of the goal, through no particular fault of your own. But wherever you begin, however far you get, and whatever obstacles you meet along the way, I sincerely believe these ideas will make you far better off financially than you would have been without them.

Remember that True Wealth has far less to do with the number of dollars you possess than the amount of freedom they provide. There will always be someone who earns a bigger salary than you or amasses a larger investment portfolio. But *time* is the great equalizer, and the greater number of days you can wake up with absolute control over how you spend them, the wealthier you are. All your life you've been told that time is money, but I hope you can see that in truth, *money is time*.

I lay no personal claim to whatever you have discovered to be new or distinctive ideas within these pages, nor do I consider myself a source of any original wisdom. But I followed this very path and completed this same journey myself, and my family and I have now made helping others—both directly and indirectly—our life's work. We try to put these concepts into practice every day and share with others what has worked.

One thing I noticed very early on is that intelligent people seem to know *what* to do. Clever people can figure out the best *ways* to do it. But successful people are the ones who actually *start doing it*—and never stop.

My wish is that you find wisdom here, apply it daily, and reach a point in your life where whatever days lie before you are yours to spend as you choose. And once you succeed, I pray that you will selflessly share what you've learned and the wealth you've created to improve the lives of those you love.

May you wake up every morning with something to look forward to, spend each day learning something new, and go to bed each night with one more thing to be thankful for.

Such is the meaning of True Wealth.

SOURCES OF WISDOM

ALAN ABELSON was a financial journalist whose "Up and Down Wall Street" column in *Barron's* magazine offered a clever and sometimes controversial perspective on the inner workings of the investment world.

CLIFF ASNESS is an investment manager known for his academic work in the field of quantitative investing and risk management.

WILLIAM BERNSTEIN is a neurologist, financial writer, and staunch proponent of index investing.

TOM BODETT is an author, voice actor, and media personality. He is perhaps best known for being the national spokesperson for Motel 6 since 1986, ending commercials with "I'm Tom Bodett for Motel 6, and we'll leave the light on for you."

JOHN C. BOGLE was the founder and chief executive of The Vanguard Group. His investment philosophy centers on low-cost index mutual funds, the first of which he is credited with creating in 1975. His legions of followers are known as "Bogleheads."

WARREN BUFFETT is quite possibly the most successful investor of all time. Known as the "Oracle of Omaha," Buffett is the chairman and CEO of Berkshire Hathaway. While he has never written a book, his timeless wisdom has spread widely throughout the investment community for decades.

W. E. B. DU BOIS was an American historian, sociologist, author, and civil rights activist. He was one of the founders of the National Association for the Advancement of Colored People (NAACP).

BEN CARLSON is a portfolio manager and author known for his popular blog, *A Wealth of Common Sense*, and several books on saving, investing, and personal finance.

WINSTON CHURCHILL was a British statesman, prolific writer, and renowned political leader. He served as prime minister of the United Kingdom during World War II and again in the early 1950s.

MARTIN H. FISCHER was a German-born physician and author. Another of his quotes is often recited to first-year medical students: "A doctor must work eighteen hours a day and seven days a week. If you cannot console yourself to this, get out of the profession."

BENJAMIN FRANKLIN was one of the founding fathers of the United States and a signer of the Declaration of Independence. His endless curiosity brought him fame as a writer, scientist, inventor, diplomat, printer, publisher, and philosopher.

SOLOMON IBN GABIROL was an 11th-century poet and philosopher.

JOHN KENNETH GALBRAITH was an economist, diplomat, and author of four dozen books and thousands of articles and essays. He also served as the U.S. ambassador to India during the Kennedy administration.

THOMAS GIBSON was a prolific writer and author best known for his investment classic *The Facts About Speculation*, written in 1923 and based on a study of thousands of brokerage accounts. He believed that emotional excesses are the root cause of most investment errors.

JOHANN WOLFGANG VON GOETHE was a German poet, playwright, and novelist of the late 18th and early 19th centuries.

BENJAMIN GRAHAM was a professor, author, and investor and is known as the father of value investing. His books *Security Analysis* (co-authored with David Dodd) and *The Intelligent Investor* are required reading for securities analysts—and for his most famous student, Warren Buffett.

JOEL GREENBLATT is a value investor, hedge fund manager, and author of *The Little Book That Beats the Market*.

NAPOLEON HILL was an author best known for his book *Think and Grow Rich*, written in 1937, which is among the 10 best-selling self-help books of all time.

MORGAN HOUSEL is an award-winning financial author, best known for his book *The Psychology of Money*, which has been translated into 46 languages. He is a partner at The Collaborative Fund, a venture capital firm.

PETER LYNCH is an investor, philanthropist, and former mutual fund manager. His mantra "invest in what you know" was popularized in his best-selling books, including *One Up on Wall Street*, and he remains widely quoted in the financial press.

HOWARD MARKS is an investment manager and author. He cofounded Oaktree Capital Management and is well known in the investment community for his "Memos" on investment strategy, the economy, and investor psychology.

PAUL MERRIMAN is a financial educator, advisor, speaker, and author of numerous books on personal finance, including *Live It Up without Outliving Your Money*.

J. P. MORGAN was a financier and investment banker who dominated American finance during what came to be known as the Gilded Age.

NICK MURRAY is a retired financial advisor and is widely considered one of the financial services industry's most respected writers and speakers.

ISAAC NEWTON was one of the world's most renowned mathematicians and physicists of all time. His discovery of gravity and the laws of motion made him one of history's greatest scientific minds.

CARL RICHARDS is director of education for the BAM Alliance, a community of U.S. wealth management firms. He is best known for his ability to illustrate complex financial concepts through simple sketches.

JIM ROHN was an entrepreneur, author, and motivational speaker. He became a millionaire at age 30, lost his entire fortune by age 33, and later became a millionaire again.

JEREMY SIEGEL is an author and finance professor at the Wharton School of the University of Pennsylvania. His book *Stocks for the Long Run* is considered a modern-day investment classic.

LEO TOLSTOY was a Russian author best known for his novels *War and Peace* and *Anna Karenina*.

MARK TWAIN is the pen name for Samuel Clemens, who was a writer, humorist, and lecturer. He was the celebrated author of dozens of short stories and novels, including *The Adventures of Tom Sawyer* and its sequel, *Adventures of Huckleberry Finn*, both considered classics of American literature.

JASON ZWEIG writes on investing and personal finance for *The Wall Street Journal*. He also edited a revised edition of Benjamin Graham's classic text, *The Intelligent Investor*.

APPENDIX:
True Wealth—A Recap

What follows is a summary of the True Wealth process, with a few more nuggets of wisdom scattered along the trail.

TRUE WEALTH IS YOURS TO DEFINE. It's the point in your life at which you no longer have to work for money, because the money you've saved and invested is now doing most of the work for you. There is no "retirement number," no "ideal retirement age," and no "optimal income level" that determine when you've earned the right to live your life the way you choose. You make the rules and decisions, and then it's up to you to live by them.

SPEND LESS THAN YOU EARN. This is the essential lifelong habit that makes True Wealth possible. Save 15% of every dollar you earn, and make it the first bill you pay every month. It's the fuel that gives compounding its immense power, and it's absolutely essential to building wealth.

IT'S NOT WHAT YOU MAKE; IT'S HOW YOU SPEND. Once you've established a regular savings habit, you must find creative ways to live the fullest life possible with the remainder of each paycheck. Prioritize your spending in each category, starting with your biggest expenses. This concept works regardless of how much money you earn or how little.

KEEP YOUR MOAT FULL. Your first financial goal is to accumulate the equivalent of 30% of your annual gross (pretax) income in a low-volatility, liquid investment vehicle. This emergency fund acts as a moat to prevent unexpected short-term expenses from derailing your long-term plan. If you ever need to tap it, divert all of your regular savings deposits into it until it's full again, and keep topping it off as your income increases over time.

GET OUT OF DEBT AND STAY OUT OF DEBT. If you have any debts other than a mortgage, direct an additional 5% of your annual gross income toward paying them off. Make the minimum payments on all of your debts as part of your regular monthly spending, and then apply the extra 5% of your income to whatever loan charges the highest rate of interest. Pay off your debts one at a time until they're all gone and make it a regular practice to pay the balance in full each month thereafter. Then you can think about paying down your mortgage, with a goal of being completely debt free before you stop working.

BE AN OWNER, NOT A LOANER. Equities are one of the few forms of investment that capture the ongoing innovation, ingenuity, and progress created by the free enterprise system. Build a portfolio of 25 high-quality, financially strong, growing businesses that consistently pay dividends and increase them faster than the rate of inflation. Endeavor to buy shares of these companies at attractive valuations.

VOLATILITY IS OPPORTUNITY DISGUISED AS RISK. One of the downsides of owning equities is that their day-to-day prices are unpredictable and often volatile. This discourages many investors who make the mistake of confusing volatility with risk, when in fact volatility is one of the reasons equities have historically delivered higher returns than more stable investments. Volatility creates the temporary discounts and premiums that allow buyers *and* sellers to take advantage of market conditions.

> "Volatility is only a risk if you have the wrong response to it."
> —BEN CARLSON

Use volatility to help you build wealth through dollar-cost averaging, and don't let short-term uncertainties distract you from pursuing your long-term objectives.

Price and risk are directly related. A new investor sees the price of her stocks *decline* and believes her risk is *increasing*. A novice sees a *rising* market and thinks risk means getting into it later than his friends. Wise investors know it's really just the opposite in both cases. Perhaps the greatest risk of all in equities is in not owning them.

> "The intelligent investor realizes that stocks become more risky, not less, as their prices rise, and less risky, not more, as their prices fall."
> —JASON ZWEIG

Feel the fear but avoid the panic. Market downturns are natural and normal, and in the long run, they have little power to harm you, unless of course you choose to let them. For that reason, it's been said that bear markets are when stocks are returned to their rightful owners.

But we don't invest in markets. We buy shares of well-run, profitable, growing *businesses*. If bear markets allow us to purchase them at undervalued prices, so much the better.

> "If you expect to be a net saver during the next five years, should you hope for a higher or lower stock market during that period? Many investors get this one wrong. Even though they are going to be net buyers of stocks for many years to come, they are elated when stock prices rise and depressed when they fall."
> —WARREN BUFFETT

It's okay to be concerned, even afraid, when stock prices appear to be falling endlessly, but the mistake you must avoid is *acting* on those fears, giving in to the panic you naturally feel. You can avoid turning a temporary downturn into a permanent loss of capital by remembering that: (1) bear markets are temporary; (2) your spending money wasn't invested in stocks to begin with; and (3) in theory, you should own shares of businesses that hopefully possess the ability to continue increasing their dividends, even when their share prices are down.

When you lose, don't lose the lesson. The only way to truly learn about investing is by investing. That means making your own decisions and your own mistakes, with your own money, and choosing to accept the consequences of those decisions. Thankfully most of your errors of judgment will come early on, when you have less at stake financially. Therefore, the sooner you start investing and making mistakes, the sooner you will learn and the longer you will have to profit from them. And it's even better when you can learn from the mistakes of *others*, so never stop reading, listening, and learning.

Don't time the market. Einstein called compounding humankind's greatest invention, but this most powerful force can be easily stopped in its tracks by any investor who believes he or she can accurately and consistently predict the short-term movement of stock prices. Why doesn't market timing work? Because it requires finding a rational approach to predicting the irrational behavior of human beings. If you insist on finding this out on your own, I encourage you to give it a try—but only after rereading the preceding paragraph. Better yet, you could simply find a consistently successful market timer and follow his or her advice to the letter. In that case, I wish you luck in your search for such a person. The rest of us will be here when you get back.

Don't invest with borrowed money. Investing with money that doesn't belong to you can enhance your profits and magnify your losses; in both cases, you are paying compound interest to someone else for the privilege. Leverage turns investing into speculation and greatly increases risk. It puts you on the clock and adds pressure, neither of which is conducive to long-term success. It adds complexity to your financial life and turns you from a tortoise to a hare. We both know how that turns out.

Keep it simple. I believe that most of what financial success entails can be explained to a five-year-old on the back of a napkin. But that will never stop some folks from trying to dazzle you with endless charts, graphs, and formulas full of Greek letters, because they know that *complexity creates the illusion of sophistication*. It could also be that they're not smart enough to make the ideas they're selling understandable. Or maybe those ideas weren't worth understanding to begin with.

True Wealth isn't easy to attain, and it doesn't happen quickly. It comes from having a belief in yourself and in the future, mastering a handful of relatively simple fundamentals, and having the discipline to put them into practice.

It's not all about knowing what to do but *doing what you know.*

AUTHOR'S NOTE

The information contained in this book does not purport to be a complete description of the securities, markets, or developments referred to in this material. The information has been obtained from sources considered to be reliable, but we do not guarantee that the foregoing material is accurate or complete. Any information is not a complete summary or statement of all available data necessary for making an investment decision and does not constitute a recommendation. Any opinions of the author are those of the author and not necessarily those of RJFS or Raymond James. Expressions of opinion are as of the initial book publishing date and are subject to change without notice.

Raymond James Financial Services, Inc., is not responsible for the consequences of any particular transaction or investment decision based on the content of this book. All financial, retirement, and estate planning should be individualized as each person's situation is unique.

This information is not intended as a solicitation or an offer to buy or sell any security referred to herein. Keep in mind that there is no assurance that our recommendations or strategies will ultimately be successful or profitable nor protect against a loss. There may also be the potential for missed growth opportunities that may occur after the sale of an investment. Recommendations, specific investments, or strategies discussed may not be suitable for all investors. Past performance may not be indicative of future results. You should discuss any tax or legal matters with the appropriate professional.

The hypothetical illustrations are not intended to reflect the actual performance of any particular security. Future performance cannot be guaranteed, and investment yields will fluctuate with market conditions.

Matching contributions from your employer may be subject to a vesting schedule. Please consult with your financial advisor for more information.

Like traditional IRAs, contributions limits apply to Roth IRAs. In addition, with a Roth IRA, your allowable contribution may be reduced or eliminated if your annual income exceeds certain limits. Contributions to a Roth IRA are never tax deductible, but if certain conditions are met, distributions will be completely income tax free.

Contributions to a traditional IRA may be tax deductible depending on the taxpayer's income, tax filing status, and other factors. Withdrawal of pretax contributions and/or earnings will be subject to ordinary income tax and, if taken prior to age 59½, may be subject to a 10% federal tax penalty.

Bond prices and yields are subject to change based upon market conditions and availability. If bonds are sold prior to maturity, you may receive more or less than your initial investment. There is an inverse relationship between interest rate movements and fixed-income prices. Generally, when interest rates rise, fixed-income prices fall, and when interest rates fall, fixed-income prices rise.

Investors should consider the investment objectives, risks, charges, and expenses of an exchange-traded product carefully before investing. The prospectus contains this and other information and should be read carefully before investing. The prospectus is available from your investment professional.

The Dow Jones Industrial Average (DJIA), commonly known as "The Dow" is an index representing 30 stocks of companies maintained and reviewed by the editors of the *Wall Street Journal*. The S&P 500 is an unmanaged index of 500 widely held stocks that is generally considered representative of the U.S. stock market. The NASDAQ Composite is an unmanaged index of securities traded on the NASDAQ system. Indices are not available for direct investment. Any investor who attempts to mimic the performance of an index would incur fees and expenses that would reduce returns.

Dollar-cost averaging cannot guarantee a profit or protect against a loss, and you should consider your financial ability to continue purchases through periods of low price levels.

Rebalancing a nonretirement account could be a taxable event that may increase your tax liability.

Dividends are not guaranteed and must be authorized by the company's board of directors.

Brokered Certificates of Deposit (CDs) purchased through a securities broker and held in a brokerage account are considered deposits with the issuing institution and are insured by the Federal Deposit Insurance Corporation (FDIC), an independent agency of the U.S. government. FDIC deposits are insured up to $250,000 per issuer (including principal and interest) for deposits held in different ownership categories including single accounts, joint accounts, trust accounts, IRAs, and certain other retirement accounts. The deposit insurance coverage limits refer to the total of all deposits that an account holder has in the same ownership categories at each FDIC-insured institution. For more information, please visit fdic.gov. About liquidity: Funds may not be withdrawn until the maturity date or redemption date. However, brokered CDs are negotiable, which means that, although not obligated to do so, Raymond James and other broker/dealers presently maintain an active secondary market at current interest rates. Market value will fluctuate and, if the CD is cashed out prior to maturity, the proceeds may be more or less than the original purchase price. Holding CDs until term assures the holder of par value redemption. CDs are redeemable at par upon death of the beneficial holder. FDIC insurance does not protect against market losses due to selling CDs in the secondary market prior to maturity.

Bond ladders are a time-honored investment technique in which an investor blends several bonds with differing maturities, providing the benefit of blending higher long-term rates with short-term liquidity. Should interest rates remain unchanged, increase, or even decline, a laddered approach to fixed-income investing may help reduce risk, improve yields, provide flexibility, and provide shorter-term liquidity. Risks include but are not limited to: changes in interest rates, liquidity, credit quality, volatility, and duration. There is an inverse relationship between interest rate movements and bond prices. Generally, when interest rates rise, bond prices fall, and when interest rates fall, bond prices rise. Diversification does not ensure a profit or protect against a loss. Investments are subject to market risk, including possible loss of principal.

Drawbacks to bond ETFs include the possibility of high expense ratios, which are the fees the investor pays the manager. Low returns are possible on this type of investment, and there are no guarantees of principal.

ACKNOWLEDGMENTS

It's a rare person who can thank his family and his coworkers in the same sentence, but such is my good fortune. I am blessed to come to work each day with the people I love more than anything on earth. My wife, Tammy, left a successful career to join my financial practice 25 years ago. It became a true family affair in 2007, when our only child, Adam, joined us in business. Our little family grew larger when Adam married Vicki Viefhaus in 2016. Our practice grew once more when Vicki joined us the following year. And our family grew again with our beloved grandchildren, Michael and Cece.

With me, it's hard to tell where my life's work leaves off and my life's joy picks up—and I wouldn't have it any other way.

I am indebted to Tammy, Adam, and Vicki—and also to the newest member of our team, Melanie Wood—for carefully reading this book and offering helpful suggestions before I sent it to the publisher. They were all there when logic, clarity, brevity, and grammar collided, and I thank them for helping me pick up the pieces.

My sister, Betty Brown, has waited most of her long life for me to write a good book, and I certainly hope she is not disappointed by my efforts. Betty has been a constant source of encouragement and support in every facet of my life, and I can never repay her love and guidance.

And patience! Same goes for Peggy Hanley, who has been a beloved member of my family longer than I have.

I learned long ago that there are things you can do on your own and things that ought to be left to people who can do them better. It's true for creating and managing wealth, and, trust me, it's true for writing a book about it. I am grateful to my friends at Greenleaf Book Group who've gotten this book into your hands: Lindsey Clark, Leah Pierre, Joan Tapper, Jordan Smith, Justin Branch, Mimi Bark, Kristine Peyre-Ferry, Amanda Marquette, Danielle Green, and Sam Ofman.

Several years ago, Brown Family Wealth Advisors selected Raymond James as our dedicated partner because we believed it was the firm best qualified to help us serve our clients, and our decision seems to get validated almost every day. In particular, I wish to thank Katie Hagan, in our home office, for helping me navigate the maze of industry rules and regulations that govern how financial advisors communicate their advice to clients and the public. This is an amazing firm to work with.

And finally, let me express my gratitude to the hundreds of clients and families we have worked with over the past three decades. In the early days, many of those I worked with were *twice* my age. They made the difficult decision to trust me with their finances, their futures, and their legacies, and it's a responsibility my family and I have never taken lightly, nor for granted.

Today, I seem to work with more and more clients who are *half* my age. Their circumstances are different from those of their parents and grandparents, but their needs are much the same. They want to feel informed, educated, and appreciated. They want a proven process—such as the one in this book—that can help them along toward their goals, regardless of where they are in life. And most of all, they want to work with someone they feel they can trust.

My family and I come to work each day in hopes of being capable stewards of your wealth and worthy of the faith you place in us. And we hope to do so for the generations still to come. Thank you for that opportunity.

ABOUT THE AUTHOR

MIKE BROWN is the founder and president of Brown Family Wealth Advisors, a wealth management practice based in St. Louis, Missouri. He and his team manage more than $400 million (as of December 31, 2021) for private clients in 23 states following fiduciary standards. Mike has held the CERTIFIED FINANCIAL PLANNER™ designation since 1992 and the Chartered Retirement Planning Counselor℠ designation since 1999. He also holds Series 7, 63, and 65 securities licenses.

Mike has been a household name among St. Louis residents for nearly four decades. He hosted the popular "News 4 Your Money" segment on KMOV-TV from 1986 to 1994. Since then, he has hosted *The KMOX Money Show*, one of KMOX Radio's longest-running and most popular *At Your Service* programs. He also wrote an investment column for the *St. Louis Post-Dispatch* for several years.

In his personal time, Mike enjoys reading, woodworking, and an occasional (when coerced) round of golf. But most of the time, you'll find him with Tammy, his wife of 42 years, and their family.